HAND KNITS FOR THE HOME AND GARDEN

HAND KNITS FOR THE HOME AND GARDEN

Alison Dupernex

THE CROWOOD PRESS

First published in 2018 by
The Crowood Press Ltd
Ramsbury, Marlborough
Wiltshire SN8 2HR

www.crowood.com

British Library Cataloguing-in-Publication Data
A catalogue record for this book is available from the British Library.

ISBN 978 1 78500 455 1

Acknowledgements
Grateful thanks are due to Rowan Yarns for keeping up with my demands for
yarn. I thank Knoll Yarns for sponsoring the Aran-patchwork blanket and Chris
Birch for help with the knitting. Also, thank you to Sharon McSwiney, jewel-
ler and metal worker, and Gilly, from Yew Tree Gallery, who allowed me to use
their gardens, in sunny Cornwall, to photograph some throws. Huge thanks
to Simon for reading and making sense of the hieroglyphs. I have had some
wonderful support.

Typeset by Jean Cussons Typesetting, Diss, Norfolk
Printed and bound in India by Replika Press Pvt Ltd

CONTENTS

INTRODUCTION

It is a very human characteristic to want to create something, and the act of creation in turn is hugely satisfying.

This book is to be used as a catalyst for your ideas. There are patterns, but the hope is that you will be inspired to adapt these or make up your own, gaining in confidence and knowledge. Colour is talked about at great length, as it is the use of colour that raises a great deal of work above the ordinary.

The joy of making some furnishings is that you do not have to get too hung up on sizing and gauge/tension. For many of the projects, such as blankets, throws and runners, it really is not important if the finished result is a few centimetres larger or smaller than the sample. However, accurate sizing is important when making a box covering or a cushion cover, because exact dimensions are required for these items to be functional.

Head, heart and hand

These three aspects are the basis on which all design is created.

Your head asks logical questions. What colours should I use? What is my project? What stitch pattern should I use? What are the likely problems that I may encounter? How will I solve them? This also covers the practical side of the design and how it will be worked.

OPPOSITE: Textured and Fair Isle blankets.

Your *heart* triggers emotions and feelings, leading to further design questions. Why should I use a certain colour? Can I not experiment and take a risk? Is my experiment successful? How tactile is my project: is it smooth and soft or bobbly and crunchy? Which options will work best for my design?

Your hand is how you can obtain the results required, by the execution of the project. Your hands are the tools for the job, and what wonderful tools!

You are standing on the shoulders of giants, and many well-known knitters have explored and developed the techniques that you will use as a keystone for further creative development.

The history of humankind has been and still is a violent one; yet, while one section of humanity is prepared to behave in utterly inhuman ways, there is another that has quietly continued to develop their practice and build on their skills as creative makers. Your philosophy of making feeds a calm, meditative core, which is hugely satisfying, and this philosophy will run through your veins like a life blood and help to make the world a more civilized and contemplative place.

In recent years, there has been a resurgence in the practice of hand knitting, and there are many reasons to explain why. The hectic pace of life requires moments of calm, and knitting, being portable and requiring just two sticks and some wool, is an ideal way of achieving this. Knitting is versatile and, when it is being performed, a calming rhythm is built up. There are no boundaries, and a pattern can be followed closely, stitch by stitch, or the maker can take flight and add stitches and change colours. Your confidence grows, and you will invent new techniques.

Seascape deckchair cover.

Even with the finest yarn, it is the quality of your design and technique that will make a work of beauty. Do not be anxious or reluctant to unpick your mistakes and start again, because this is all part of the learning process and will pay dividends in terms of your completed design. Some mistakes can be happy accidents, but not all, so do not be afraid to experiment!

Bring your knitting to life by always considering how it can be made better, and experiment with innovative details, because this will extend your skills.

With the head, heart and hand all employed, knitting really does become a therapeutic and creative experience; many knitters have known this for generations, but for others it is a new understanding.

A short history of knitting

The true history of knitting is lost in the mists of time, but there are early examples from the Near East. Fragments of knitted textiles, socks, to be precise, have been found in Egyptian tombs, and these were knitted in the round and feature two colours of yarn. They have been dated between 1200BC and 1500BC and show that the knitters of that time were making practical items and designing their own stitch patterns, echoing intricate woven-carpet borders.

Rare examples have also been found in Spanish tombs, dating from the thirteenth century: they are exceptionally finely worked, with intricate two-colour patterns showing a strong Arabic influence, and a gauge/tension of twenty stitches per 2.5cm (1in). Many of the early examples have survived because they were made for occasional liturgical use.

Historically, knitting was a male craft. During the European Middle Ages, a knitter's apprenticeship was served over three years, and another three years of travel was undertaken to explore and learn new patterns and techniques. The degree of refinement attained was exceptional, and, to become an accredited knitter and join a guild, which was essential to gain work, an exam had to be passed. A number of original 'masterpieces' had to be designed and knitted in a short time: a felted cap, a pair of stockings or gloves with a decorative pattern, a shirt or waistcoat, and a carpet or hanging of 183cm × 152cm (6ft × 5ft), to show off the skill of patterning flora and fauna. The mind-boggling intricacy required indicates that these items may have been made on a knitting frame. Only when this process was completed and passed did the knitter become a master. The intricate and exquisite garments were worn by members of the nobility, and each had his own favourite master.

There is evidence from England to suggest that complex knitted caps were made in Coventry during the thirteenth century, such as the Monmouth cap: this was worked with stocking stitch being knitted with four needles, and the rough, coarse wool was then felted. This style of cap was still being made in the nineteenth century for soldiers engaged in the Crimean War. The makers of these garments were called Cappers and worked full-time for the production of these caps.

Finely decorated hose were fashioned for men to show off their legs, and the English monarch Elizabeth I is said to have imported knitted silk stockings from Spain. The demand in Tudor times then grew for finely knitted garments, and pantaloons were also made with slashes to reveal not only lace patterns but delicate knit-and-purl patterns.

In his book *A History of Hand Knitting*, Richard Rutt discusses the colour of men's stockings in France in the early seventeenth century. He cites evidence in a satirical novel of the time that mentions wonderful, evocative shades such as Dying Monkey, Merry Widow, Resuscitated Corpse and Sad Friend! There are examples of hose in shades of pink and beige, which would fit with these descriptive and expressive names.

Hose became an important fashion statement during the seventeenth century, depending on whether they were made from wool or silk, with those hose made from silk being perceived to belong to wearers of higher social status than those made from wool. The colour of the hose also had great significance, and members of Oliver Cromwell's Parliament of 1653 were called 'blue stocking' as a term of abuse. Later, blue and grey became unfashionable, because they had puritanical overtones. Over a century later, ladies clubs too were called blue stocking after scholar Benjamin Stillingfleet appeared at one of Elizabeth Montagu's assemblies wearing blue worsted stockings, instead of the more socially acceptable white silk. The term is still used today in an unflattering way, to describe an educated, intellectual woman.

Many hundreds of knitters were employed making hose, so it was not popular when, in 1589, a curate by the name of William Lee devised the first stocking-frame knitting machine to speed up the slow manufacturing process. The English monarch Elizabeth I refused him a patent twice, and she expressed her concern that many of her subjects would become beggars and the skills of the artisans die out. This backlash was instigated by the Hosiers Guild whose job it was to protect the livelihoods of the sock and stocking makers. After one disastrous partnership, William Lee went into another with his brother and moved to France, where the French monarch Henry IV granted him a patent. He found success for a few years, having started up an industry in Rouen; however, with Henry's assassination in 1610, Lee's fortunes plummeted. He died in 1614 in penury.

Lee's brother, James, returned to England and started a partnership with a previous apprentice of William's, and two centres were established, one in London and another in Nottingham, to produce knitted hose using the industrialized framework-knitting process. During the eighteenth century, there was fierce competition between the centres in Leicester and Nottingham as to who was the leader of this industry.

Although it took nearly a hundred years, a thriving industry using wool, silk yarn and knitted lace fabric was established in England. The machinery that Lee developed was hugely important and created a firm foundation for the textile industry for many years to come.

King Charles I of England is said to have been executed while wearing a delicate knit-and-purl-decorated silk shirt. Many garments of this era were made with two colours of thread, one of which was metallic, used specifically to imitate jacquard woven fabric.

The Worshipful Company of Framework Knitters was granted a charter in 1657 under Oliver Cromwell, but machine knitters were no real threat to hand knitters for at least another two hundred years, because hand knitting was both fast and cheap. It was only with the introduction of man-made fibres and the increase in the demand for knitted fabrics that hand-knitting jobs were threatened.

A Dutch knitted wool petticoat dating from the eighteenth century can be seen at the Victoria and Albert Museum in London; measuring 317cm (125in) in circumference and with a depth of 76cm (30in), it is covered with geese, alligators, rhinoceroses, wild boar, dogs and myriad other animals worked entirely with knit and purl stitches. No animal is repeated, and there are approximately 2,750 stitches per round. The detail and finesse of the work is such that it would not be possible to technically produce a work of this calibre today, because of the loss of skill.

Lace knitting had been popular in Europe since the fifteenth century, when silk yarn became more widely available. The action of knitting two stitches together and yarn over (yo) makes a small hole and, when knitted with a fine silk yarn, can create beautiful, delicate openwork scarves, gloves and hose. Lace knitting continued to grow in popularity. When, during the eighteenth century, cotton and muslin threads were imported from the East, the fashion was for 'white knitting'; this was produced using thread, finer than sewing cotton, knitted with fine wires and on the thinnest of needles. At this time, aristocratic ladies worked the most exquisite examples of white knitting in the form of samplers, and, by the mid-eighteenth century, knitting had become a pastime, not a necessity, and was practised by all social classes.

While this revolution was taking place, in the rural counties knitting was being developed and practised by country folk as a way to make money. Whole families worked on knitting garments for sale, because knitting was easy to pick up and put down, and all the tools were readily available and inexpensive. Each member of the family was expected to make a pair of hose a week. Women, men and children would all walk, herd, and talk as they knitted. A yarn rattle would be wound into the centre of a ball of wool so that the ball could be found in the winter months if it rolled into a dark corner. Sailors and fishermen developed their own patterns; it was the women's task to spin the yarn, and the men, whose nimble fingers were used to knotting nets and tying ropes, were the knitters.

The men of the Aran Islands developed their own unique patterns, and today the Aran sweater has become a generic term for a cable-knit garment.

Very often, a deliberate mistake was inserted into the pattern, as the culture was deeply religious, and nothing was supposed to be perfect except for God.

It is often thought that families had their own stitch patterns, and how the pattern was placed in relation to another pattern denoted where the sweater came from and even who had knitted it, which could prove to be useful information. If the wearer of a sweater fell overboard and was washed ashore, they could be identified based on the sweater's stitch patterns; however, this is sadly an urban myth, but it is such a romantic idea that it is still often repeated as fact.

As the colonial expansions of Britain and other European countries gained pace, the skill of knitting as practised in Europe spread to other parts of the world. In America, boys and girls went to knitting school to learn to make socks and gloves, and, during the American Civil War, it was seen as patriotic to knit comforts for the troops. Missionaries also spread the craft to China and Japan, and the practitioners in these countries have become experts in this field.

At the beginning of the nineteenth century, knitting yarns became softer, following the introduction of merino wool. As yarns became more widely available, the mechanized framework knitting machine became ubiquitous. Knitting was no longer exclusively thought of as a craft of the poor but as part of the first Industrial Revolution.

Middle-class ladies, however, continued to make exquisite beaded purses, mufflers, shawls and even dresses. It was during this time that many of the patterns that are used today were incorporated into the canon of work: Fair Isle patterns, Aran cables and patterns, Shetland lace, and the Scandinavian-colourwork lice patterns, to name but a few.

Towards the end of the nineteenth century, commercial knitting patterns began to be published, and magazine issues were brought out monthly to encourage knitters to make a variety of items from toilet-roll holders in the shape of a poodle to intricate twisted-stitch jackets. In 1906, abbreviations such as 'ss' for stockinette stitch were first used.

In the nineteenth century in the Shetland Islands, wool was spun into the finest of threads and worked into delicate shawls, which it was said could pass through a wedding ring. Queen Victoria and other members of the royal family were seen wearing these shawls, which sealed their popularity. Queen Victoria was herself a knitter and 'recipes' were published to fuel the interest in knitting: patterns for bags, pin cushions, baby clothes, shawls and many other accessories were made available, with some examples being technically sophisticated. Tension and needle size were not the issues that they are today; what was important to the knitter then was the practicality of how to make the garment and the stitch pattern.

There was a complete explosion of knitting in the home during the First World War. Patterns were adapted, and parts of different patterns were incorporated into single pieces of work: it was a real melting pot. Wives, mothers and sweethearts knitted gloves, hats and many other items to be sent to their loved ones in the conflict areas, because this provided comfort and solace to both the knitter and the soldier.

Around the same time, in India, paisley designs were used as motifs on caps; in South America, hats and leggings were made that emulated indigenous woven designs; and all over the world hats, gloves, sweaters and coats were made, with each nation having its own particular signature motif. In the British Isles, the wealthy aristocracy saw the home production of knitted garments as a way to keep the street urchins from the workhouse.

In the early twentieth century, the English aristocracy also encouraged the knitting industry of the Shetland Islands, by wearing the sweaters produced there and so making them fashionable. Edward, the Prince of Wales, famously wore a Fair Isle sweater; he had his portrait painted by John St Helier Lander in 1925, showing this garment, which he had worn to the opening of the golf season at St Andrews golf course, Scotland, in 1921. The bright pattern of the sweater reflected the jazz age and was picked up by Coco Chanel, and its place in history was assured. The unique and distinctive character and vibrancy of the pattern meant that it was highly adaptable and has never been out of fashion.

Fair Isle designs featured natural colours found in sheep's wool; later, natural dyes of browns, soft greens, ochre and indigo were all used, up until the Second World War. Then, the background colour began to change, making rich stripes of Fair Isle and bands of

Knitting from around the world.

subtle wave patterns in colours of similar shades that were placed at the top and bottom of OXO patterns, which added to the intricacy and originality of each garment.

The first recorded cable-knit sweaters were made in the early twentieth century on the Irish Aran Islands of Inishmore, Inishmaan and Inisheer, and they were made fashionable in the 1960s by the author Heinz Edgar Kiewe, who wrote *The Sacred History of Knitting* in 1967. He found a creamy white sweater with cables, twisted stitches and bobbles in Dublin in 1936 and became a passionate advocate of this style of garment and the techniques involved in the production of these sweaters.

Many other patterns were created over the years, and moss stitch, trellis stitches and small and large cables all add to the unique style of the cable-knit sweater. There has been and continues to be much discussion as to the true origins of this garment, but the techniques and style appear to be relatively recent. By 1954, there were many examples of this distinctive patterning, and it has brought welcome work to the people of the Irish islands. The cable-knit sweater has been popular since its first discovery and has never fallen from favour, which demonstrates the enduring, attractive quality of the stitches.

New techniques are being developed all the time, and one such example is mosaic knitting, advocated by designer Barbara Walker. The interplay between slip stitches, knit and purl stitches, and various colour changes produces a distinctive, textured fabric when using this technique.

The fortunes of hand knitting have waxed and waned, even though the expensive, leading fashion houses have constantly kept knitting in their collec-tions: Elsa Schiaparelli made the iconic sweater with a trompe l'oeil bow in the 1920s, Coco Chanel has repeatedly used panels and blocks of knitted fabrics in her designs from the 1920s onwards and, post-2000, Vivienne Westwood has crafted clinging lace panels, delicate flowers and Fair Isle patterns, all on the same garment. Knitting is a truly versatile medium that will continue to be used, because it allows makers to produce designs that are fashionable, exciting and innovative.

As a reference, small pieces of knitting can be collected, and there are various fairs and vintage sales that you can visit to buy these treasures. Sadly, many older pieces have been lost because of moth damage.

The featured little waistcoat from Pakistan, worked with cotton, has the most eye-catching and vibrant colours: note the innovative use of a zip for the edging. The Peruvian hat, while more sober in colour, is extremely finely knitted, using traditional patterns.

By having a better understanding of the historical perspective of how knitting has developed, you can better appreciate the rich diversity of the designs that you can create through the application of the different influences that inform and inspire your work.

This first chapter has introduced you to some of the key ideas that go together to create good knit-ting-design practice, and my hope is that you will be inspired to assimilate and adapt these ideas on your design journey, gaining in confidence and knowledge, to produce work of exceptional quality.

Making knitted furnishings allows you to have great flexibility in the design process, with your flair and imagination at the forefront.

Please use the designs and ideas presented in this book as inspiration for your own projects.

CHAPTER 1

YARNS AND TOOLS

Yarns

No amount of excellent knitting will increase the quality of inferior yarn. There are many varieties of yarn available; whether your preference is for wool, cotton or silk yarn, or a yarn featuring a combination of materials, there will be a good choice available. All of the above yarns are spun from a fibre, and how they are spun will indicate the finished look of the yarn and knitted fabric. The fibres are all spun from filaments or staples. Filaments can be continuous in length and are mainly synthetic, the only exception being silk. Staples are shorter, and the spun yarn is made up of many short strands. The longer-staple merino wool and Egyptian cotton spin into smooth, good-quality threads.

All fibres fall into two categories: natural or synthetic.

A variety of yarns.

Natural fibres

These are subdivided into two categories: animal proteins and vegetable cellulose.

Animal proteins include mohair, wool, alpaca, cashmere, angora and silk fibres.

Vegetable cellulose includes flax (linen), cotton, sisal, hemp, bamboo and jute fibres.

Sadly, moths love all animal fibres, and their larvae feed off the proteins that these fibres are made of. If it is suspected that the yarn or knitted fabric has been attacked by moths, place it in the freezer for two weeks; this will kill any larvae.

OPPOSITE: Textured throw in the rugged landscape that inspired its design.

Synthetic fibres

Yarns made from synthetic fibres such as nylon, acrylic and polyester were primarily developed and popularized after the Second World War. They are made from a variety of mineral sources, the main exception being viscose rayon (or artificial silk), which is derived from cellulose and was developed in 1894 by the English chemists Charles Frederick Cross and Edward John Bevan.

The yarn that you select will determine the finished quality and character of your project. Most yarns are denoted by their count number (or thickness). The standard system in use today is the 'new metric' (Nm) system.

The Nm count number indicates the length in metres of one gram of yarn. So, for instance, 1g of 11Nm yarn will be 11m long, and 1g of 1.6Nm yarn (aran weight) will be 1.60m long.

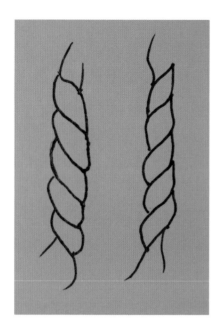

Diagram of S and Z twist.

Under this system, two ends of 1.6Nm yarn placed together would be equivalent to a single yarn of 0.8Nm. When yarns in lengths are twisted together, they are denominated as 'ply', and two-, three- and four-ply indicate how many lengths of yarn have been twisted or plied together within each yarn. The Nm count number indicates the length per gram of yarn: the lower the Nm count number, the thicker and heavier the yarn and the smaller area of fabric that you can knit per gram of the yarn.

The choice of needles depends on how firm or loose the resultant fabric needs to be. So, an average knitter working with aran-weight yarn could use a 5.5mm (US9, UK5) needle, but a tighter knitter could use a larger 6mm (US10, UK4) needle to obtain the same results. Your needle selection is an indication of the weight of the fabric being produced, combined with the tightness of your knitting.

Spinning twists the staples or filaments together into a spiral; a twist to the left is called an S twist and to the right is called a Z twist. The resultant spirals of yarn can then in turn be further twisted together to be plied into a thicker, stronger yarn.

Yarns spun from wool are either worsted or woollen. Worsted yarn is spun from longer staples that are combed to make the fibres lie straight against each other, in parallel, which produces a firm feel for the resulting yarn. To produce woollen yarn, wool fibres are carded, to clean and untangle the shorter fibres, and are then rolled into a loose sausage shape, which is then drawn into a yarn by spinning. Woollen yarn is not as strong as worsted yarn.

Bamboo, sari fabric, paper, ribbon and many other variations of yarn are available for you to work with.

There are also many different finishes to yarns; for example, 'superwash' yarn can be washed in a washing machine and subsequently be dried without the yarn shrinking, and mercerization adds strength and lustre to cotton.

Dyeing yarns can produce a solid colour, and different textures and mixes of colours can be created in the spinning process by combining other yarns and tufts of fibres to give a different character to the finished yarn.

Space-dyed yarns are randomly dyed in different colours and can produce interesting effects when knitted; however, when working with this type of yarn, it is best to change the balls of yarn every few rows and then change back again, repeating this process throughout the knitting of the fabric, to avoid having a sunburst effect in your work.

There is, however, not a standard specification that yarn manufacturers adhere to, and each country has its own methods of describing the thickness and qualities of yarn. The accompanying table will be useful in helping you to obtain the appropriate yarn and needle size to knit a particular design.

Yarn weights		Recommended needle sizes		
UK	US	Universal (mm)	US	UK*
Four-ply	Sport	3	2–3	11
Double-knit	Light worsted	4	6	8
Aran	Fisherman	5	8	6
Chunky	Bulky	6	10	4
Super-Chunky	Extra bulky	9	13	00

* Note that the UK needle sizes are no longer manufactured

Table listing equivalent yarn weights and recommended needle sizes.

Ball bands

Almost all yarn will have a ball band, and the information provided there is invaluable, especially if you are intending to experiment with felting or other techniques. It contains the advised gauge/tension and needle size; however, this is only a guide, and, with the projects in this book, you do not need to stick to it. The stated fibre content of the yarn will need to be known if you intend to try felting, and the ball-band symbols or text should inform you about washing instructions for the yarn and the resulting knitted fabric. If the yarn does not have a ball band and you need to establish whether the yarn contains wool, with a match, set fire to the end of a length of yarn, blow out the flame and sniff. If there is a burnt, acrid smell, the yarn is probably made of wool, but, if the end has retreated into a little melted ball, it is synthetic yarn.

Substituting yarns

At times, when a yarn that you want to use in your project is no longer available, it may be possible to find an equivalent yarn to use instead.

Think about the characteristics of the original yarn; how it was textured and what the colour and its fibre content were are all considerations to take into account, or an allergy to wool may make it vital that the fibre content of the substitute yarn will be different from that of the original yarn.

The only way to be sure that your substitution gives the effect that you are after is to knit a swatch and compare the gauge/tension, appearance and feel of the fabric to those of the original fabric, then adapt the pattern to suit the substitute yarn. Also think about the stitches that you are using: with a delicate knit-and-purl pattern, do not use a space-dyed or heavily variegated yarn, otherwise the stitch pattern will be lost.

Look to experiment and incorporate your own ideas into the patterns in this book. Try adding texture and colour by using three or four differently coloured strands of yarn to add a twist to the design. Explore design options by using several different knitting techniques within a pattern; the designs that I have created are a template for you to experiment with.

The resulting swatches of yarn and technique experimentation are never wasted and, when sewn together, will be an archive of your creativity. If the swatches are different sizes, cut out a paper template of the smallest block. Pin the template to each of the larger swatches in turn, marking around the template edges and machine stitch around the markings twice. The swatch fabric to the outside of the stitching lines can then be trimmed off without the stitches unravelling. The machine stitching will be hidden in the seam when the blocks are later sewn together.

Tools for the job

Needles

The basic tools used for knitting are your needles, and great care should be taken over their selection.

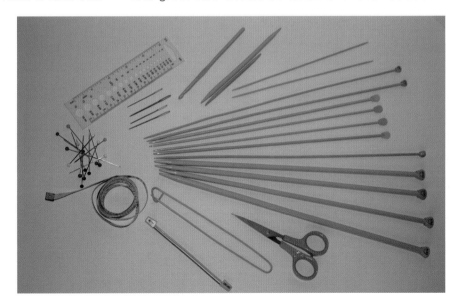

Tools for the job.

There are two categories of needle: straight and circular.

Straight needles can be made from aluminium, plastic, bamboo or wood. Bunches of needles can be purchased from charity or thrift shops, but these are often not the bargain that they appear to be, as bent and damaged tips will slow down the action of knitting and snag yarn. Wooden needles are slower to use, as the yarn does not slide off the needle tips and along the needle shafts as well as for needles made from materials with smoother surfaces, but with use they gain a warm patina from the oils in wool yarns and from hands. Experiment to see which needles and materials suit you best. If you take care of your needles, they will give a lifetime of reliable service.

Circular needles can have advantages, especially when working on larger projects. These needles are more balanced to use, because the stitches will automatically slide to the middle, are easier to use in a constricted space, and take up less room. They can also be used in the same manner as a straight needle, with the work being turned at the end of each row.

Needle sizes

All needles come in a range of sizes and lengths, and the size denotes the needle diameter. This diameter can be expressed in metric and US sizes, and some needles state old UK sizes, as listed in the accompanying table. The old UK size needles are no longer manufactured; however; many needles whose sizes are expressed by this system are still in use, so details have been included for easy reference.

Universal (mm)	US	UK
2	0	14
2.25	1	13
2.75	2	12
3	–	11
3.25	3	10
3.5	4	–
3.75	5	9
4	6	8
4.5	7	7
5	8	6
5.5	9	5
6	10	4
6.5	–	3
7	–	2
7.5	–	1
8	11	0
9	13	00
10	15	000
12.5	17	–
15	19	–
19	35	–
20	36	–

Table listing equivalent needle sizes. Please note that the equivalents are approximate: where they fall between sizes, dashes have been shown.

Cable needles

Also known as double-pointed needles (dpns). They are available in a variety of sizes, and you should always use a size smaller than your main knitting needles for a project, to keep the cable tight.

Needle gauge

These are helpful for any needles that are not marked with their size. Some needles are not true to size, so sizing can be checked using your needle gauge.

Stitch holder

To hold a couple of stitches, you can use a standard safety pin, but, for more stitches, you can purchase a version made specifically for knitters. For a long row of knitting that you may need to take off your needles, it may be easier to thread the stitches temporarily on to a length of contrast-colour yarn.

Sewing needles

Use blunt-tipped tapestry or darning needles of various sizes for sewing up garments. Such needles are

Colouring pencils and graph paper for designing your own projects.

also required for the Swiss darning of decoration: this is an embroidered stitch (also known as duplicate stitch) that mimics and covers the original knitted stitch (*see* Appendix for instructions to work this embellishment). The tip should be blunt rather than sharp; a sharp tip can split the yarn, and the results will be untidy. A bodkin may also be useful for drawing decorative threads through fabric knitted on larger needles or that has a textured surface, for embellishment.

Pins
Quilting pins are the best to use, because they are longer, with coloured heads, and so are easier to see among the knitted stitches.

Tape measure
This should be marked with both centimetres and inches. Fabric tape measures can distort and stretch; fibreglass tape measures are the best choice, as they will keep their shape and not react to temperature changes.

Scissors
The most useful scissors are small and pointed. My advice here is to buy the best that you can afford, because cheap scissors are often a false bargain.

Graph paper
Standard square-grid graph paper will distort the proportions of the knitted stitch, which is not square, so use knitter's graph paper, which has grids that represent different gauges/tensions. The knitter's graph-paper blocks are rectangular to better represent the shape of the knitted stitch.

Most knitted fabric works up to a ratio of 4:5: the width of four stitches is the same as the height of five rows. Thicker yarn will have a different ratio, but you can ascertain this by working a tension swatch. There are various knitting sites on the internet from which you can download and print knitter's graph paper in a variety of ratios.

Abbreviations

3-st BC   sl 1 st to the dpn and hold at the back of the work, k2, then p1 from the dpn.

3-st F   sl 2 sts to the dpn and hold at the front of the work, p1, then k2 from the dpn.

BC   back cross. When cabling, this means that the dpn holding cable stitches is left in position at the back of the work while the other stitches that are part of the cable are worked.

C2B   sl 2 sts to the dpn and hold at the back of the work, k2, k2 from the dpn.

C2F   sl 2 sts to the dpn and hold at the front of the work, k2, k2 from the dpn.

cm   centimetres

dec   decrease

DK   double-knit

dpn   double-pointed needle or cable needle

FC   front cross. When cabling, this means that the dpn holding cable stitches is left in position at the front of the work while the other stitches that are part of the cable are worked.

g   grams

in   inches

inc   increase

k   knit

k2tog   knit two stitches together as one stitch (a one-stitch decrease).

knitwise   insert the RH needle tip into the front leg of the indicated stitch as if it is to be knitted (from the front of the work, from left to right). This instruction is often used to describe how to slip a stitch from one needle to the other.

LH   left-hand

No   number

p   purl

p2tog   purl two stitches together as one stitch (a one-stitch decrease).

p3tog   purl three stitches together as one stitch (a two-stitch decrease).

psso   pass the slip stitch over. Insert the tip of the LH needle into the slip stitch, and lift it up and over the stitch that has just been knitted, over the tip of the RH needle and off the needle (a one-stitch decrease).

purlwise   insert the RH needle tip into the front leg of the indicated stitch as if it is to be purled (from the front of the work, from right to left). This instruction is often used to describe how to slip a stitch from one needle to the other.

rep   repeat

rep from *   repeat all of the instructions after the first * of the row or of the preceding line(s) of instruction.

RH   right-hand

RS   right side of the work

sl   slip. Pass a stitch (stitches) from the LH needle to the RH needle without working it (them). Stitches can be slipped knitwise or purlwise: purlwise is the default method, and a pattern should specify occasions when slipping knitwise is required. Stitches that have been slipped are referred to as slip stitches.

sl1–k2tog–psso   slip a stitch knitwise (sl1), knit the next two stitches together as one stitch (k2tog) and pass the slip stitch over (psso) (a two-stitch decrease).

ssk	slip, slip, knit. Slip the first and second stitches knitwise, one at a time, from the LH needle to the RH needle. Insert the tip of the LH needle from the left into the fronts of the two stitches now on the RH needle, and knit these two stitches together (a one-stitch decrease).
st	stitch
sts	stitches
st st	stocking (or stockinette) stitch. Knit across one row (or specified stitches) and purl across one row (or specified stitches) alternately, when knitting with a pair of straight needles.
tog	together
WS	wrong side of the work
wyib	with yarn in back. This is used with slip-stitch patterns. When the stitch is slipped, the yarn is carried across behind the stitch, away from the knitter, on the reverse side of the work, as the stitch is slipped.

wyif	with yarn in front. This is used with slip-stitch patterns. When the stitch is slipped, the yarn is carried across in front of the stitch, on the front of the work, close to the knitter.
yo	yarn over. From the front of the work to the back of the work, take the yarn over the top of the RH needle once before working the next stitch.
(yo) twice	perform the yarn-over manoeuvre twice, to create a double yarnover on the needle. From the front of the work to the back of the work, take the yarn over the top of the RH needle twice before working the next stitch.
*	repeat the instructions after the asterisk or between two asterisks as many times as indicated in the pattern.
()	a pair of parentheses indicates the instructions written within that are to be repeated as many times as indicated in the pattern.

CHAPTER 2

TECHNIQUES AND STITCHES

Tension swatches and gauge

The tension swatch is very important when following patterns or designing your own patterns, as it provides you with the vital information that you need in order to achieve the correct dimensions and feel of the fabric for your finished item. Gauge is expressed as the number of stitches and rows per centimetre (or inch), which are measured from your tension swatch. You then only have to multiply the stitch pattern enough times to reach the required width and length to determine how many stitches to cast on and work for the particular item. After you have done this several times, you do begin to get a feel for the number of stitches and rows required for a particular size or feel of fabric, and this will broaden with your experience.

The standard gauge/tension that I have stated for my knitting of the patterns in this book may well be different to the tension that you achieve for your knitting. To make allowance for this, the needles that you use may need to be adjusted to a smaller or larger size, to obtain the correct gauge/tension for the pattern.

Yarn substitution can also affect tension, and you will need to make a small tension swatch first to ensure that the dimensions of the knitted pattern will be correct; if you make the swatch large enough to measure 10cm (4in) square, then you should generally have no problems with determining the gauge of the tension swatch. Sometimes, however, it is necessary to make even larger tension-swatch squares, especially when designing with cables and cable-stitch patterns, which tend to pull in the fabric.

Casting on

Every knitter has their own favourite cast-on technique, but, if the cast-on is too tight, try using a larger needle. The cast-on techniques that I have used in this book are the thumb method and the cable method.

Thumb method

The thumb method of casting on requires one needle.

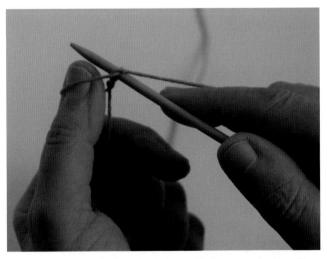

Leaving a long tail of yarn, make a slip knot on the needle, which is held in the right hand. Wrap the yarn tail around the thumb of the left hand, and insert the needle up through the loop on the thumb.

OPPOSITE: Box covered with textured and colourful slip-stitch fabric.

Wrap the yarn from the ball over the needle, pull this wrapped yarn through the loop with the tip of the needle and gently tighten the stitch that has been formed. Repeat this process until all of the required stitches have been cast on.

Cable method

The cable method requires two needles, and this technique forms a firm, neat edge.

Make a slip knot on the LH needle, and cast on one stitch by following the thumb method. Insert the RH needle between the slip knot and the first cast-on stitch on the LH needle.

Casting off (binding off)

When you have been working a stitch pattern and the time comes to cast off, keep to that pattern: knit the knit stitches and purl the purl stitches as you cast off. If you tend to cast off too tightly, use a larger needle.

To make a neat last stitch that will not extend and look out of shape, cast off until one stitch remains on the LH needle, and slip this stitch purlwise on to the RH needle. Insert the point of the LH needle into the stitch one row below the slip stitch. Return the slip stitch to the LH needle, and knit the picked-up loop and the slip stitch together. Pull the yarn through the last stitch to complete the cast-off.

Wrap the yarn from the ball around the RH needle, and pull through this wrapped yarn between the slip knot and the first cast-on stitch with the tip of the needle, to make a new stitch on the RH needle. Gently tighten this stitch, and place it on the LH needle in the orientation shown. Repeat this process by inserting the RH needle between the two cast-on stitches closest to the tip of the LH needle, until all required stitches have been cast on.

Charts

Charts are used for Fair Isle and intarsia patterns (for an overview of these techniques, see the sections 'Fair Isle' and 'Intarsia' later in this chapter, as well as patterns throughout this book). Rows on the front of the work (RS) should always be read from right to left and rows on the back of the work (WS) from left to right (unless otherwise stated in the pattern). Where the pattern that is being produced is worked with stocking stitch, the front rows of the work are knitted, and the rows on the back of the work are purled.

Finishing

Take time with this process, as it will enhance the appearance and overall quality of a piece of knitting. Many beautiful projects have been ruined by sloppy sewing-up and the knitter not bothering to block and press the knitted fabric.

Finishing typically involves the two-stage process of blocking and pressing, whereby the fabric is first blocked, to achieve the required dimensions, and then pressed, to give the fabric a professional finish.

Blocking

Knitting can distort and have a twist to it, especially when large pieces are worked. This can be rectified by pinning out and pressing (blocking) to achieve a particular fabric shape. If the size of the knitted fabric has turned out to be slightly smaller than hoped for, the fabric can be gently stretched, pinned and pressed. Uneven knitting, various lumps and bumps, and rolled edges can be smoothed after knitting: do not underestimate the power of a good press under a damp cloth during blocking.

Only block and lightly steam-press garter stitch (formed by knitting every row, when knitting with straight needles) and knitted bobbles, because full pressing would flatten out these textured fabrics.

A blanket or towel can be used as a surface when blocking your work, although the best thing to use is a heat-resistant fabric that is made to protect tables. Cover this with a cotton sheet. Lay the work over the top of this fabric and, with reference to a tape measure, adjust to the measurements of the knitted piece

as required. Make sure that the knitted rows run parallel to each other. Pin the work at intervals, and gently spray the knitted piece with water to moisten the fabric. Leave the pinned-out fabric undisturbed while you wait for it to dry: this will take time, possibly a day or more.

Pressing

Once the fabric has been blocked, you can press the fabric to obtain a professional finish. Check the yarn ball band to ascertain whether the manufacturers advise against pressing the fabric once the yarn is knitted up. As a guide, man-made yarns such as acrylic should not be pressed, because they tend to go limp and lose their shape. Wool, cotton and silk mixtures can be lightly pressed.

There are two ways of achieving a good press. One method is to cover the work with a damp cloth lying over the knitted piece (as described above for blocking, where the intention was to achieve particular dimensions for a piece of knitted fabric), and use an iron on a normal heat setting, working the iron gently over the piece. The other method is to use a dry cloth and the iron set to produce steam. Do not drag the iron across the knitted fabric, because this will distort the work: a gently back-and-forth, horizontal, waving motion of the iron is all that is required. Allow the work to dry thoroughly before removing the pins.

Mattress stitch

This is an almost invisible stitch that is used to sew seams, to join the edges of knitted pieces of fabric.

Having blocked and pressed the fabric pieces, place the two edges to be seamed together side by side, thread a needle with a length of seaming yarn and secure the end of this length of yarn to the work so that it emerges through the fabric, from the back of the work to the front of the work, at the very bottom corner of one of the pieces.

With the needle above the fabric, insert it down to the back of the work between the first and second stitches at the bottom edge of the other piece of fabric,

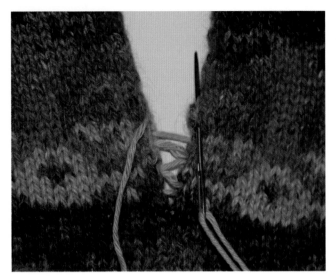

Mattress stitch being worked.

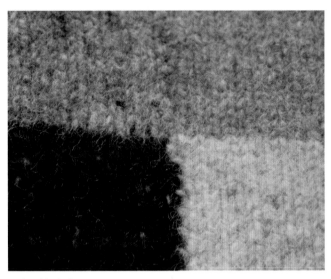

Felted knitting.

run it under two ladders between the first and second columns of stitches and take it up to the front of the work between the first and second stitches two rows above the bottom edge of the fabric.

Take the yarn across to the opposite piece of fabric, and match the sewing steps performed for the corresponding stitches and rows on the other piece (inserting the needle down to the back, running it under two ladders and taking it up to the front as stated).

Continue back and forth, moving up the pieces of fabric two rows at a time, gently drawing them together by gently pulling on both ends of the seaming yarn periodically, until the seam is complete.

Other stitches are used to join cast-on and cast-off edges, attach separately knitted edgings and create other seams for knitted fabric. Where a particular stitch or method should be used, guidance often will be given in the pattern.

Felting

This process changes the characteristics of the fabric and makes it denser and firmer, with less-defined stitches.

The yarn must be made of wool fibres, otherwise it will not felt! Try out felting a test swatch of a known number of stitches and rows before you start knitting the actual piece; this will help you to decide what dimensions of fabric you need to knit. Felting can be done by hand washing the knitted fabric, but my preferred method is to make use of a washing machine, as described next.

How well a knitted fabric felts will depend on the temperature of the water, the duration of the wash, the level of agitation and the spin speed. After lots of experimenting with my washing machine, I have found that a 40°C wash, for one hour, with a spin speed of 800rpm, gives a medium felt effect. For a much lighter felt, I use a 30°C wash, for forty minutes, with an 800rpm spin speed.

A faster spin will result in a matted fabric, which can be just what is needed, but I like the fabric to have a certain amount of drape. These are just guidelines from my experiences with my washing machine; you will need to experiment with your own machine to work out what is the correct programme to give the effect you are looking for.

Stitch patterns and colour

Many of you will have more than one knitting project in progress at any one time, usually a straightforward one and also one or two that could take years to complete.

Every piece is a journey: exciting, meditative and problematic and, most importantly, it is part of your own creative development.

Basic stitches

All stitches are based on knit and purl; these are the building blocks. It is time well spent really getting to know what all the variations are, which include slip stitches, twisted stitches, cabled stitches, lace stitches and many more.

Stocking stitch is the canvas of the designer, and it is the surface on which to overlay line, shape, colour and texture. By adding any or all of these effects, the work will rise from being mundane and average into a piece of striking, crafted art.

Stitch and colour variations.

Colour

When choosing colours, decide what it is that appeals to you; this in itself is an act of discovery. Allow the time to look at things in detail and depth, and this will broaden the design experience and add to your understanding.

The physical material used, the yarn, and its texture, ply, mix of threads and colour will all work together to create an energetic, sculptural fabric. Certain colours and stitches can trigger a recognition or a memory. This is a tangible effect, as the fabric can be touched,

wrapped around you, stroked and felted, so your knitted fabric becomes a truly sensual experience.

Colours, patterns and techniques used before can re-emerge years later and be used in a different way, informed by all of the projects worked in between. Often, there will be a consistency that will become your signature style, as a favourite colour, stitch or felting technique emerges.

Think about what colours and shapes are brought to mind when considering places and emotions. For example, the setting sun over the sea, the reds and purples of the sky and the clouds in flame, with the moon reflected in the water, all trigger thoughts of stripes and circles outlined with a darker colour, taking your breath away.

Many designers have been moved by musical references, calm spaces with intricate, complex patterns of movement in between, so why not write a symphony with yarns, by using stitch and colour. Overlapping stitches and colour can facilitate merging and leaping of movement, which crackles with energy. Vigorous stripes and curvilinear slip-stitch patterns can morph into cables and, in turn, geometric Fair Isle patterns.

Use rhythmic and pulsating colours such as red and yellow, and emerald green and bright purple. Experiment, and always be open-minded to changing your original design. Colours and patterns can be knitted with one aspect in mind and metamorphose into a different significance. Round moon shapes in a night sky over a misty sea can change into snowberries on a hoar-frosty morning.

This is when informed experimentation can take flight. Soft, pale, pastel berries can change in colour into summer berry fruits such as black, red and white currants, raspberries and strawberries, which can change into bright balloons. Add colours and take some away until there is a dynamic balance.

Design considerations

Informality in your designs is fine, but this must be underpinned by excellence of craft and technique. The choice of stitch pattern dictates which threads are taut and which more relaxed; space is created by soft, plain areas set against, say, an intricate stitch knitted with a marled yarn, which will change emphasis and break the rhythm. For example, try adding a splash of amber to navy blue, and, to amethyst purple, try adding a line of brown, as this creates a surprising contrast. There are no boundaries, apart from your imagination.

A basic stocking-stitch fabric can be brought to life by adding other yarns, texture and, of course, colour. Try out swatches of texture and colour, and keep them safe to refer back to when making future designs. When blocked and pressed, they can be stitched together to make a throw: nothing should ever be wasted!

Patterns can be altered, divided and made larger or smaller. There are always new patterns and variations to explore, and this will extend your knitting vocabulary and also enable a new confidence to knit more creatively. Layer pattern upon pattern: offset lace and cables, and twisted stitches and colourful Fair Isle: enjoy painting with the threads.

Depending on the stitch pattern that is employed, slip stitch, tuck stitch, or two-colour Fair Isle, try putting cherry red with leaf green, or china blue with marmalade orange, or violet with maroon, or turquoise with olive green: these are all colours that will pulsate against each other to create a dynamic in the design. For a quieter fabric, why not try using shades of grey such as charcoal, steel or dove.

The artist Winifred Nicholson made her own colour chart using her own evocative names to describe the colours that she used, from light to dark, providing link to both time and place in her memory. For blues, the lightest shade is Shadow, getting darker through Mist, Sea Grey, Air-Force Blue, Fell Blue, Turquoise, Azure, Baby-Ribbon Blue, Sky, Forget-Me-Not, Larkspur, Lapis Lazuli and Horizon, finally reaching the darkest shade, Zenith. This works for me, so why not try using names for your yarns that describe the colours in a way that is more relevant to you, as your descriptions

Yarn drying outdoors at Plockton, Harris.

Shades of cream.

can then evoke memories and feelings that you can incorporate into your creative process, to personalize your designs.

Shades of cream can create a dramatic fabric, and nothing is better than Aran cables and twisted stitches creating a furrowed landscape of pebbly bobbles, travelling ropes, honeycombs and other exciting textures. This style is utterly timeless and inspirational; it not only brings to mind the fishermen and their wives who designed the patterns, and their tough lives, but also is awe-inspiring from the use of minimal colour to create maximum richness of the fabric.

Many stitch patterns lend themselves to colour experimentation; slip-stitch and Fair Isle patterns are ideal candidates. A rigid plan is not necessary, especially when making throws, blankets and cushions.

To check whether a colour variation is working well, I find it helpful either to look at the fabric in a mirror or take a photograph of it and then view it that way. If the tones and shades are too close together, meaning that the pattern will be lost, this will easily show up, and, contrariwise, if there is a glaring colour that dominates and unbalances the others, it will become clear and can be rectified at an early stage.

Fair Isle

True Fair Isle comes from Spain and uses only certain patterns that are based on the Armada cross; however, the term Fair Isle has become generic and now describes a particular pattern and technique. Fair Isle knitting can change colour from stitch to stitch, but only two colours are used in a row. Traditional Fair Isle was worked on a circular needle, so no purl rows would be worked. A sweater would be worked in the round, and armholes and a neck opening would be cut into the knitted fabric. One particular kind of Fair Isle knitting from Sweden is called Bohus knitting. This knitting style originated from an initiative started in the 1930s

Fair Isle knitting.

to provide work for the women of the stone-quarrying districts of Bohuslän who faced unemployment and extreme hardship. It has a very distinctive look and uses myriad colours, with knit and purl stitches alongside the colour changes.

Most Fair Isle patterns today are made up of small patterns repeated across the work, using the basic stocking stitch, by knitting one row and purling the next, when working with a pair of straight needles.

To keep the work neat on the reverse, stranding can be used for small pattern repeats; the unused yarn colour is carried lightly across the back of the knitting, and any new yarn colour is picked up from underneath the yarn colour being dropped, to prevent holes appearing in the finished piece. The yarn colour not in use is called the floating yarn, and, if the requirement is for this yarn to be carried across more than five stitches on the back of the work, it is usually better to weave it in. The floating yarn is woven over and under the working colour of yarn until it needs to be used again. Whether the unused yarn is stranded or woven in, a double layer of yarns is created, so Fair Isle knitting makes for a thicker fabric, ideal for a blanket or throw. Whichever way of working is chosen, stranding or weaving in, it is vital to keep the tension even, otherwise puckering will result.

Designing for Fair Isle is relatively easy, as each stitch can be represented by an oblong in your design grid. With the aid of colouring pencils, wonderful, intricate designs can emerge, and you can allow your imagination to take flight.

Intarsia

Intarsia is the technique that is used when blocks of colour are worked by knitting with separate balls or lengths of yarn. The yarns are not carried across the back of the work, but, at the boundaries of blocks of colour, the yarn that has just been worked is twisted around the next yarn colour to be worked, to avoid a hole.

When using many different colours, to avoid getting the different yarns tangled up, either cut off shorter lengths of yarn to work with, and keep pulling them through each other to separate them as you work, or wind longer lengths of yarn around separate bobbins.

Roses worked with intarsia.

Intarsia knitting is worked from a chart, as with Fair Isle patterns. Designing for intarsia is relatively easy: work with graph paper where each oblong in your design grid represents a stitch of the fabric.

Lace

The basis for a lace stitch pattern is a hole, formed by working the steps of knit two together (k2tog) and yarn over (yo). The arrangement of these holes produces a particular lace fabric.

Lace knitting.

Cables

Cables are formed from twisted stitches, which create wonderful decorative effects. All of the traditional stitch patterns represent an aspect of the fisherman's life and surroundings, from which the stitch patterns were originally devised when they were being applied in the making of sweaters. For example, the little knobbles of the bramble stitch are hedgerow berries, the crossed cables are the ropes criss-crossing on the boats, and the shadow cable represents the patterns left on the sand after the tide has gone out.

Dry bones, twin wave, drunken sailor and homes of Donegal are all descriptive names for cables that conjure up in the imagination a way of life. There are, however, many differing stories as to what each cable

Knitting featuring cables and bobbles.

represents. Each coastal area and family had its own particular variations, and these were altered when marriages took place, when stitch patterns were combined and customized.

The Aran Islands, off the western coast of Ireland, became well known for their combinations of stitches used in knitted fabric, and other areas with seafaring populations, including Cornwall, Yorkshire, Guernsey and Jersey and many coastal towns, also added to this rich encyclopedia of stitches. Families also worked special-occasion garments, such as marriage sweaters.

The fashion industry has repeatedly used these delightful patterns to innovative and inspiring effect. However, because of the popularity and wearability of these sweaters, many cheap versions are now made by machines and with larger needles, for speed; they are a sad replication of the originals, passed off by unscrupulous sellers as handmade. Placed side by side with the originals, there is no comparison in terms of the quality of the finished work or the integrity and authenticity of the design.

A cable is achieved by using a dpn to hold some of the cable stitches at the back or the front of the work while the other stitches that are part of the cable are being worked. The number of stitches that are held on the dpn and whether those stitches are held to the front or back of the work determine the thickness and direction of twist of the cable, respectively.

Twisted stitches

These stitches are produced by twisting stitches around each other to form a twist resembling a cable, without using a dpn. The technique is to skip the stitch closest to the point of the LH needle and to knit the adjacent stitch, leaving it on the needle, then to knit the skipped stitch, after which both stitches are dropped off the LH needle. Twisted stitches are sometimes referred to as mock cables, because the resulting pattern looks like a cable but a cable needle is not used to work the stitches.

Fun can be had making the stitches travel left or right. As with all twisted and cabled stitches, the fabric is pulled in horizontally, so it is advisable to make a tension swatch. Beautiful, delicate, barley twist cables can be made with this versatile stitch.

Twisted stitches.

Mock-cable stitches.

Slip stitches

Slip-stitch patterns are one of the most interesting stitches, and the most wonderful, energetic results can be achieved with this technique. It is an easy stitch to master, and many variations can be experimented with.

The method is straightforward; a stitch is slipped from the LH needle to the RH needle, while the working yarn is held either behind or in front of the stitch being slipped.

In some slip-stitch patterns, the yarn is always held behind the stitch, so the yarn does not show on the front of the work (an example of this is shown in the heel-stitch illustration in this book). In other slip-stitch patterns, the yarn is carried across the front of the work, and this, combined with multiple colour changes, can produce a 'close', rich fabric. In this case, the slip stitch is knitted on the next row, which pulls up the work and produces a denser effect: this is called close fabric.

As a rule, the stitch should always be slipped purlwise, so that it is not twisted when it is worked on

Slip stitches.

the next row. However, sometimes a pattern will state to slip the stitch knitwise, where a twisted stitch is required.

Intricate single-colour fabrics can be worked, which have a firm and lightly textured feel (see the section 'Dishcloths and facecloths' in Chapter 8 for patterns); nevertheless, adding colour really enhances the appearance of this stitch.

Interesting results can be created by using different sizes of needles and lots of colour changes. Small, intricate, tweed-like patterns can morph into larger, bold, solidly coloured, mosaic tessellations (see the section 'Covered boxes' in Chapter 9 and the various colourwork patterns throughout this book). This is a really under-used stitch, and for the most part undervalued too, but it is one of the stitches that I use most in my work.

CHAPTER 3

CUSHIONS AND PILLOWS

We all need warmth, from not only a physical point of view but also a psychological one. The softness and plumpness of a cushion invites us to lean back and immerse ourselves in the comfort of a woolly cloud, and what better if handmade and designed by you. I am a firm believer that you can never have too many cushions or pillows piled up on a sofa or bed or on an outdoor bench in the summer.

The following cushions are worked with Fair Isle and intarsia techniques, but look out for others in the book using different stitches; for example, the small, textured seashore cushions are designed to match the seashore runner.

Garden flowers

This is one pattern with three very different looks. A small Fair Isle pattern can be used in many different ways, by changing the colours and adding Swiss darning to embellish the finished work.

Hydrangea cushion

Soft, faded colours from the Felted Tweed range from Rowan inspired this version of the pattern.

Size
To fit a cushion pad, 30.5cm × 45.5cm (12in × 18in)

OPPOSITE: A selection of cushions.

Yarn
Rowan Felted Tweed – 1 × 50g ball each of 197 Alabaster (A), 185 Frozen (B), 194 Delft (C), 157 Camel (D) and 192 Amethyst (E)

Hydrangea cushion.

Needles

A pair of 4mm (US6, UK8) straight needles
A pair of 4mm (US6, UK8) dpns, for working an optional i-cord to finish the edge of the cushion

Extras

Cushion pad, 30.5cm × 45.5cm (12in × 18in)
Zip, 30.5cm (12in)

Tension

24 sts and 30 rows = 10cm (4in) over st st, after washing and pressing

Note

- The front and back of the cushion cover are knitted as one piece.
- Read the chart from right to left for RS (odd-numbered) rows and from left to right for WS (even-numbered) rows.
- Use the Fair Isle technique throughout, and strand the yarn across the back of the work.
- Twist yarns around each other when changing yarn colours on WS rows to avoid a hole.

X				X	X	X				X	X	X				X	X	X			X	X	5
X	X		X	X		X	X		X	X		X	X		X	X		X	X		X	X	4
	X		X			X		X			X		X			X		X			X	X		3
X	X		X	X		X	X		X	X		X	X		X	X		X	X		X	X	2
X				X	X	X				X	X	X				X	X	X			X	X	1

Garden-flowers chart.

Method

Using 4mm needles and A, cast on 90 sts. Work 1 row st st (to which the zip will be attached).

* Work 3 rows st st with A.
Work the 5-row garden-flowers chart with X = B.
Work 3 rows st st with A.
Work 3 rows st st with C.
Work the 5-row garden-flowers chart with X = D.
Work 3 rows st st with C.
Work 3 rows st st with E.
Work the 5-row garden-flowers chart with X = A.
Work 3 rows st st with E.
Work 3 rows st st with B.
Work the 5-row garden-flowers chart with X = C.
Work 3 rows st st with B.
Work 3 rows st st with D.
Work the 5-row garden-flowers chart with X = E.
Work 3 rows st st with D.
Rep from * until eighteen chart stripes, each with 3 rows of st st above and below, have been completed. Work 1 row with E, and cast off.

Finishing and making up

Sew in the yarn tails, and trim the ends.

Fold the cushion cover in half (the fold line will be between the ninth and tenth chart stripes).

With a length of one of the yarn colours, stitch together the LH edges and the RH edges to form side seams, then sew in and trim the seaming-yarn ends.

Insert the cushion pad or, using a length of sewing thread, sew in the zip to both sides of the bottom opening of the cushion cover, then sew the rest of the bottom of the cushion cover closed.

Add an extra finishing touch by making an optional i-cord over 4 sts with yarn colours C, D and E held together, as one thread (see Appendix for instructions to work this embellishment).

Cast off when the cord measures 152cm (60in), slightly stretched; this is enough cord to be placed and sewn around the entire perimeter of the cushion.

Make and add tassels (see Appendix for instructions to work this embellishment), and sew them securely to the cushion's four corners.

Winter-border cushion

A very different effect can be gained for the hydrangea cushion by a complete colour change and Swiss darning the centre of the stylized flowers. Inspiration came from the muted colours of a winter border, with brighter flashes of colour from decaying roses.

Hydrangea and winter-border cushions.

Size

To fit a cushion pad, 30.5cm × 45.5cm (12in × 18in)

Yarn

Rowan Felted Tweed – 1 × 50g ball each of 193 Cumin (A), 170 Seafarer (B), 172 Ancient (C), 150 Rage (D), 145 Treacle (E) and 183 Peony (F) for knitting the cushion cover, and 181 Mineral, only for Swiss darning the flower centres

Needles

A pair of 4mm (US6, UK8) straight needles
A pair of 4mm (US6, UK8) dpns, for working an optional i-cord to finish the edge of the cushion

Extras

Cushion pad, 30.5cm × 45.5cm (12in × 18in)
Zip, 30.5cm (12in)

Tension

24 sts and 30 rows = 10cm (4in) over st st, after washing and pressing

Method

Using 4mm needles and A, cast on 90 sts for the front of the cushion cover.

Follow the instructions for the hydrangea cushion, changing the colour sequence to A with X = B, B with X = A, C with X = D, D with X = C, E with X = F, then F with X = D.

Follow this colour sequence until nine chart stripes, and their adjacent 3-row stripes of st st, have been completed.

The back of the cushion cover is worked with 4-row stripes, using all of the yarn colours in a sequence of your choosing.

Using 4mm needles and one of the yarn colours, cast on 90 sts, and work 1 row.

Work a total of twenty-five stripes of 4 rows each, then cast off (the back piece will now measure the same as the front piece).

Add embellishment by Swiss darning the centre of each flower with Mineral.

Finishing and making up

Finish and make up as for the hydrangea cushion but, rather than folding the single-piece front and back in half, sew together the top, cast-off edges of the separate front and back pieces of the cushion cover.

Embellishment added with Swiss darning.

Yarn
Any four-ply yarn that matches the tension requirements – 11 × 50g balls, each of a different colour; for example, bright blue (A), cerise (B), yellow (C), red (D), royal blue (E,) orange (F), lime green (G), pale pink (H), sky blue (I), bright pink (J) and purple (K)

Needles
A pair of 3.5mm (US4, UK9–10) straight needles
A 3.5mm (US4, UK9–10) crochet hook

Tension
29 sts and 34 rows = 10cm (4in) over st st, after washing and pressing

Garden-flowers throw

A wonderful, exuberant, bright throw. Overflowing flower borders dictated the search for lots of clear, clashing colours of four-ply yarn. This throw has eleven colours worked into it. Gathering them all together, I found out which colours reacted best together; for example, bright blue with rich red, and fiery orange with vibrant lime green. This helped me to determine the best colour sequence for knitting the throw.

The colour sequence is fairly easy, as it was the changing colours and how the colours reacted that I wanted to convey. The X colour of the garden-flowers chart becomes the stripe colour of the next pattern repeat, and so on.

Size
Width × length, 64cm × 196cm (25in × 77in)

Method
Using 3.5mm needles and A, cast on 180 sts.
Work 3 rows st st with A.
Work the 5-row garden-flowers chart with X = B.
Work 3 rows st st with A.
Work 3 rows st st with B.
Work the 5-row garden-flowers chart with X = C.
Work 3 rows st st with B.

Garden-flowers throw.

Work 3 rows st st with C, then the garden-flowers chart with X = D, and so on.

Continue to work through the colours, and repeat the colour sequence until the fabric measures 196cm (77in) in length, finishing at the end of a pattern repeat (with 3 rows of st st).
Cast off.

Finishing
Sew in all yarn tails, and trim the ends.

Using a 3.5mm crochet hook, add a double-crochet edging using the brightest colours of yarn (*see* Appendix for instructions to work this embellishment).

Cabbage roses

Roses are a quintessential English flower: large and blousy but also fine and delicate. They are the essence of summer.

These two cushions are worked using the intarsia technique, because blocks of colour are required. Separate balls of yarn are needed for each block of colour. When the yarn colour is changed, make sure that the yarn that is about to be used is twisted around the previously used yarn colour, otherwise a hole will appear. To avoid balls of yarn becoming twisted and knotted, cut off short lengths of yarn to work with.

Size
To fit a cushion pad, 61cm × 30.5cm (24in × 12in)

Yarn
The roses on both cushions are worked using the same colours; only the background colour is different

Treacle-brown cabbage-roses cushion
Rowan Felted Tweed – 1 × 50g ball each of 161 Avocado, 158 Pine, 152 Watery, 184 Celadon, 150 Rage, 183 Peony, 185 Frozen and 186 Tawny, for knitting the roses, and 145 Treacle, for the background

Alabaster cabbage-roses cushion
Rowan Felted Tweed – 1 × 50g ball each of 161 Avocado, 158 Pine, 152 Watery, 184 Celadon, 150 Rage, 183 Peony, 185 Frozen and 186 Tawny, for knitting the roses, and 197 Alabaster, for the background

Needles
A pair of 4mm (US6, UK8) straight needles

Extras
Cushion pad (per cushion), 61cm × 30.5cm (24in × 12in)
Optional zip (per cushion), 30.5cm (12in)

Tension
23 sts and 31 rows = 10cm (4in) over st st, after washing and pressing

Cabbage-roses cushions.

Note

- The front and back of the cushion cover are knitted as one piece.
- Read the chart from right to left for RS rows and left to right for WS rows.
- Use the intarsia technique throughout.

Treacle-brown cabbage-roses cushion

Method

Using 4mm needles and Treacle, cast on 130 sts for the front of the cushion.

Starting with a knit row, work 6 rows st st.

Follow the cabbage-roses chart, following the accompanying colour key for the treacle-brown cabbage-roses cushion, until all of the chart rows have been worked.

Work 6 rows st st with Treacle.

For the striped back of the cushion, work 10-row stripes with Pine, Watery, Avocado and Celadon in turn, and repeat this stripe sequence until a total of seven stripes of 10 rows have been worked.

Cast off loosely.

Finishing and making up

Sew in all yarn tails, trim the ends, and block and press the fabric.

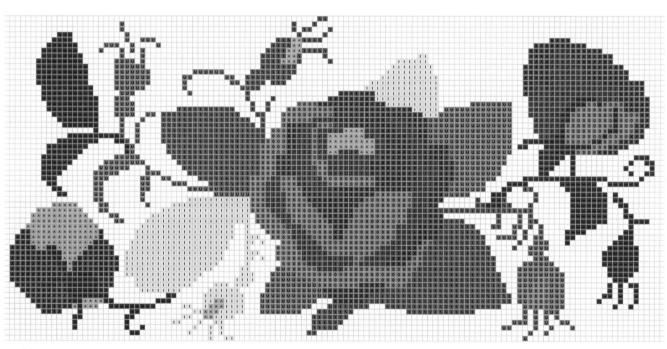

Cabbage-roses chart.

RIGHT: Colour keys for the cabbage-roses chart.

Treacle-brown		**Alabaster**	
□	145 Treacle	□	197 Alabaster
U	161 Avocado	U	161 Avocado
–	158 Pine	–	158 Pine
\	152 Watery	\	152 Watery
I	184 Celadon	I	184 Celadon
X	150 Rage	X	150 Rage
0	183 Peony	0	183 Peony
^	185 Frozen	^	185 Frozen
/	186 Tawny	/	186 Tawny

Fold the cushion cover in half (the fold line will be between the top of the charted roses pattern and the bottom of the first stripe), and stitch the two side seams.

Insert the cushion pad, and slip stitch the sides together, or place the zip where desired and stitch it in, and continue to sew together the rest of the bottom seam.

Alabaster cabbage-roses cushion

Method
For the front of this cushion, follow the instructions for the treacle-brown cabbage-roses cushion, using the accompanying colour key for the alabaster cabbage-roses cushion (the only change is that Alabaster is used for the background colour).

For the back of this cushion, again follow the instructions for the treacle-brown cabbage-roses cushion, but note that the stripes are worked with Tawny, Rage, Peony and Frozen.

Finishing and making up
Finish and make up as for the treacle-brown cabbage-roses cushion.

Design your own

A great source of inspiration is old books about embroidery, cross stitch and Berlin woolwork. They contain charts of leaves and flowers of every kind that can be used as a starting point for your own design. Pick a motif that appeals and simplify it, because blocks of colour have better impact. Lots of small details tend to be lost, and the overall effect becomes muddled. So, keep it simple.

Fair Isle cushions

True Fair Isle has no more than two colours in a row, although the intricacy of many of the patterns and colour choices can make it seem as though more colours are present. There are two ways to keep your colours neat at the back of the work.

The first method is stranding and is used when you change colour after working about five stitches. Drop the yarn colour that has just been worked to the back of the work, and pick up the next yarn colour to be worked from the back of the work, making sure that it is not pulled too tight and distorting the work. Start to

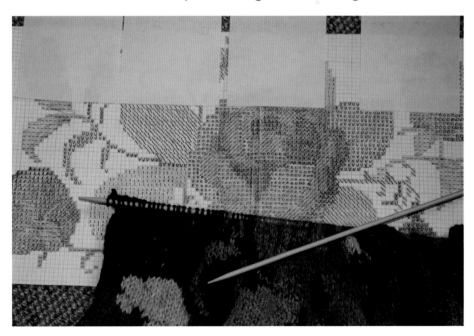

Use sticky notes to keep your place while working from a chart.

Fair Isle-and-tartan-block, Fair Isle-variation and Luskentyre cushions.

work with this colour. When stranding, the yarns not in use are said to be floating.

The other method is to weave in the yarn that is not in use (the non-working yarn); this second yarn colour is caught up by the working yarn and is therefore woven into the back of the knitted fabric. With the yarn colour being used (the working yarn) in the right hand and the non-working yarn in the left hand, bring the non-working yarn over the point of the RH needle, and knit the next stitch with the working yarn, by bringing the working yarn under the non-working yarn present on the needle. It will then go under the next stitch.

I have knitted three different cushion covers all using a traditional Fair Isle pattern, adding other smaller patterns and an Argyll pattern, and they each look

very different. I have not stipulated a particular four-ply yarn, as any Shetland-wool or Donegal-wool yarn will be perfect to use, and both types of yarn are available in a wonderful colour range. There is a rough indication of the colour used for the samples shown, but part of the process is to choose the colours to customize your own designs.

Fair Isle-and-tartan-block cushion

The front of the cushion cover is worked as two panels, a Fair Isle panel and a tartan-block panel, which are then stitched together.

The back of the cushion cover is worked in a jazzy Argyll pattern, with new colours being added and

Fair Isle-and-tartan-block cushion.

surprising colour changes through-out the knitting of the chart. However, many different colours can be added, and working this pattern is a great way to using up odd balls of four-ply yarn.

Size
To fit a cushion pad, 52cm × 30.5cm (20½in × 12in)

Yarn
Any four-ply yarn that matches the tension requirements – 2 × 50g balls each of cream, yellow, orange, pale blue and chocolate, for knitting the front of the cushion cover, and 1 × 50g ball each of red, bright blue, grey and lime green, for knitting the back of the cushion cover

Needles
A pair of 4mm (US6, UK8) straight needles

Extras
Cushion pad, 52cm × 30.5cm (20½in × 12in)
Optional zip, 30.5cm (12in)

Tension
21 sts and 28 rows = 10cm (4in) over st st, after washing and pressing

Note
· Read the charts from right to left for RS rows and left to right for WS rows.

· Use the Fair Isle technique throughout, and strand the yarn across the back of the work.

Snowflake chart.

Fair Isle 1 chart.

Tartan-block chart.

- cream
/ yellow
X orange
0 pale blue
\ chocolate

Colour key for the Fair Isle 1 chart and tartan-block chart, for the Fair Isle-and-tartan-block cushion.

Method

Fair Isle front panel

Using 4mm needles and cream, cast on 60 sts.

   * Work 4 rows st st.

   Following the snowflake chart, work the 5-row pattern with cream and \ = chocolate.

   Work 4 rows st st with cream.

   Follow the Fair Isle 1 chart, using the accompanying colour key, until all of the chart rows have been worked.

   Rep from * once, work the snowflake chart again with cream and \ = chocolate, and finally work 4 rows st st with cream.

   Cast off loosely.

Argyll chart.

Tartan-block front panel

Using 4mm needles and cream, cast on 60 sts.

Follow the tartan-block chart, using the accompanying colour key, until 101 rows have been worked (the tartan-block front panel will now be the same length as the Fair Isle front panel).

Cast off loosely.

Back

Using chocolate, cast on 120 sts, and work 2 rows st st.

Follow the Argyll chart, using the following colour sequence:

Work rows 1–24 with chocolate and X = orange.
Work rows 25–36 with chocolate and X = lime green.
Work rows 37–48 with red and X = lime green.
Work rows 49–60 with red and X = bright blue.
Work rows 61–66 with red and X = chocolate.
Work rows 67–72 with chocolate and X = yellow.
Work rows 73–78 with pale blue and X = yellow.
Work rows 79–84 with pale blue and X = cream.
Work rows 85–90 with grey and X = cream.
Work rows 91–96 with grey and X = chocolate.
Work rows 97–108 with pale blue and X = chocolate.
Work 1 row with pale blue, and cast off loosely.

Finishing and making up
Sew in all yarn tails, and trim the ends.

Wash, block and steam-press the front panels and back of the cushion cover.

Join the Fair Isle and tartan-block front panels together with mattress stitch.

Sew the two side seams and the top seam, and insert the cushion pad.

Either slip stitch the entire bottom opening closed with a length of yarn or, if desired, sew in a zip with sewing thread.

Fair Isle-variation cushion

Bright, dramatic colours create a completely different feel to that of the previous cushion. The lime green, bright red and vibrant blue fizz and crackle when placed next to each other.

The Luskentyre cushion and the reverse sides of the Fair Isle-and-tartan-block and Fair Isle-variation cushions.

The background is worked with chocolate: it creates a plain border to set off the main Fair Isle 1 pattern. The middle section of the Fair Isle 1 pattern has been revised, becoming the Fair Isle 2 pattern, worked with two colours only, for a sharper effect, and the first twelve rows of the Argyll pattern make up the middle border.

Size
To fit a cushion pad, 34cm × 34cm (14in × 14in)

Yarn

Any four-ply yarn that matches the tension requirements – 1 × 50g ball of oatmeal, 2 × 50g balls each of lime green, red, purple and bright blue and 3 × 50g balls of chocolate

These amounts are approximate, because the exact requirements depend on the specific yarns that are used

Needles

A pair of 4mm (US6, UK8) straight needles

Extras

Cushion pad, 34cm × 34cm (14in × 14in)
Optional zip, 34cm (14in)

Tension

21 sts and 28 rows = 10cm (4in) over st st, after washing and pressing

Note

· Read the chart from right to left for RS rows and left to right for WS rows.
· Use the Fair Isle technique throughout, and strand the yarn across the back of the work.

-	-	X	X	X	-	X	X	X	-	X	X	X	-	X	X	X	-	X	X	X	-	-	X		13
X	X	X	X	-	X	-	X	X	-	-	X	-	-	X	X	-	X	-	X	X	X	X	-		12
X	X	X	-	X	X	X	-	X	-	-	-	-	X	-	X	X	X	-	X	X	X	-			11
X	X	-	X	X	X	X	-	X	-	-	-	X	-	X	X	X	X	X	-	X	X	X			10
X	-	X	X	X	-	-	-	X	-	X	-	X	-	X	-	-	-	X	X	X	-	X	X	X	9
-	-	X	X	X	X	-	-	-	X	-	X	-	X	-	-	-	X	X	X	X	-	-	X		8
-	-	X	X	X	X	-	-	-	X	-	X	-	-	-	X	X	X	X	-	-	-	X			7
-	X	X	X	X	-	-	-	X	-	X	-	X	-	-	-	X	X	X	X	-	X				6
X	-	X	X	X	-	-	-	X	-	X	-	X	-	X	-	-	-	X	X	X	-	X	X		5
X	X	-	X	X	X	X	-	X	-	-	-	X	-	X	X	X	X	X	-	X	X	X	X		4
X	X	X	-	X	X	X	-	X	-	-	-	-	X	-	X	X	X	X	-	X	X	X	-		3
X	X	X	X	-	X	-	X	X	-	-	X	-	-	X	X	-	X	-	X	X	X	X	-		2
-	-	X	X	X	-	X	X	X	-	X	X	X	-	X	X	X	-	X	X	X	-	-	X		1

Fair Isle 2 chart.

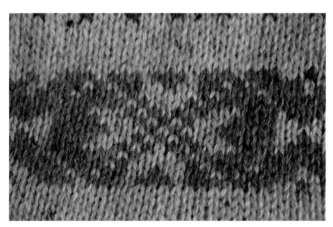

A knitted sample worked from the Fair Isle 2 chart.

Method

Fair Isle-variation front

Using 4mm needles and chocolate, cast on 100 sts, and work 2 rows st st.

Follow the Fair Isle 2 chart, using - = chocolate and X = oatmeal.

Work 4 rows with chocolate.

Follow the Fair Isle 1 chart, using the accompanying colour key, until all of the chart rows have been worked.

Fair Isle-variation cushion.

- chocolate
/ lime green
\ red
X purple
0 bright blue

Colour key for the Fair Isle 1 chart,
for the Fair Isle-variation cushion.

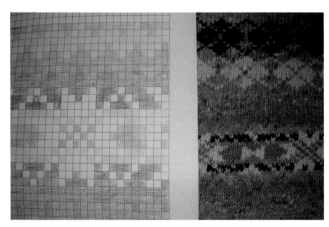

Detail of the colour chart for the Luskentyre cushion.

Work 8 rows st st with chocolate.
Work the first 12 rows of the Argyll chart using chocolate and X = purple.
Work 8 rows st st with chocolate.
Repeat working the Fair Isle 1 chart.
Work 4 rows st st with chocolate.
Repeat working the Fair Isle 2 chart.
Work 4 rows st st with chocolate.
Cast off loosely.

Back

The back of the cushion is worked by following the Argyll chart, with alternate yarn colours changing every twelve rows. You can also have fun changing the colours around, which makes for a mosaic-style pattern.

Using 4mm needles and chocolate, cast on 100 sts, and work 2 rows st st.

Following the Argyll chart, change one yarn colour every 6 rows as shown:

Work 6 rows with chocolate and X = bright blue.
Work 6 rows with purple and X = bright blue.
Work 6 rows with purple and X = lime green.
Work 6 rows with red and X = lime green.
Work 6 rows with red and X = chocolate.
Repeat the colour sequence from the beginning until 126 rows of the Argyll chart have been worked.
Work 2 rows with chocolate (the back will now be the same length as the front), and cast off loosely.

Finishing and making up

Follow the finishing and making-up instructions for the Fair Isle-and-tartan-block cushion.

Luskentyre cushion

This colour scheme is based on the colours seen during many visits made to Luskentyre beach on beautiful Harris.

The turquoise, luminous sea and soft sand yielding up small shells in pinks and blues are uplifting. The grey and cream rocks, set beside the dunes, and the little pathway that leads through them to the wild flowers are inspirational.

The Argyll chart and Fair Isle 1 chart, which have been adapted to create a more open, cream star shape, are used in stripes from top to bottom, but this time the background colour changes to add more depth.

Size

To fit a cushion pad, 46cm × 42cm (18in × 16in)

Yarn

Fine, four-ply, Donegal-wool yarn, approximately 3 × 50g balls each of cream, grey, sea blue, bright blue, pale blue and charcoal

Needles

A pair of 3.75mm (US5, UK9) straight needles

Extras

Cushion pad, 46cm × 42cm (18in × 16½in)
Optional zip, 41cm (16in)

Tension

27 sts and 36 rows = 10cm (4in) over st st, after washing and pressing

Note

- The front and back of the cushion cover are knitted as one piece.
- Read the charts from right to left for RS rows and left to right for WS rows.
- Use the Fair Isle technique throughout, and strand the yarn across the back of the work.

-	-	-	/	-	-	-	/	-	-	-	/	-	-	-	/	-	-	-	/	-	-	-	/	-	-	-	/	**31**
/	-	/	/	/	-	/	/	/	-	/	/	/	-	/	/	/	-	/	/	/	-	/	/	/	-	/	/	**30**
/	/	/	/	/	/	/	/	/	/	/	/	/	/	/	/	/	/	/	/	/	/	/	/	/	/	/	/	**29**
/	/	/	X	/	/	/	X	/	/	/	X	/	/	/	X	/	/	/	X	/	/	/	X	/	/	/	X	**28**
X	/	X	X	X	/	X	X	X	/	X	X	X	/	X	X	X	/	X	X	X	/	X	X	X	/	X	X	**27**
X	X	X	X	X	X	X	X	X	X	X	X	X	X	X	X	X	X	X	X	X	X	X	X	X	X	X	X	**26**
X	X	X	0	X	X	X	0	X	X	X	0	X	X	X	0	X	X	X	0	X	X	X	0	X	X	X	0	**25**
0	X	0	0	0	X	0	0	0	X	0	0	0	X	0	0	0	X	0	0	0	X	0	0	0	X	0	0	**24**
0	0	0	0	0	0	0	0	0	0	0	0	0	0	0	0	0	0	0	0	0	0	0	0	0	0	0	0	**23**
	0	0	0			0	0	0			0	0	0			0	0	0			0	0	0				0	**22**
	\	\	\		\		\	\			\			\	\		\		\	\	\			\	\	\		**21**
\	\	\		\	\	\		\				\		\	\	\		\	\	\		\	\	\				**20**
/	/		/	/	/	/		/			/		/	/	/	/		/	/		/	/	/					**19**
/		/	/	/			/		/		/		/			/	/	/			/	/	/					**18**
	X	X	X	X			X		X		X			X	X	X	X					X						**17**
	X	X	X	X	X			X		X			X	X	X	X	X											**16**
	X	X	X	X			X		X		X			X	X	X	X				X							**15**
/		/	/	/	/			/		/		/			/	/	/	/			/	/						**14**
/	/		/	/	/	/	/		/			/		/	/	/	/	/			/	/	/					**13**
\	\		\		\	\	\		\			\		\	\	\		\	\	\		\	\	\				**12**
	\	\	\			\	\		\			\			\	\		\	\	\			\	\	\			**11**
	0	0	0			0	0	0			0	0	0			0	0	0			0	0	0				0	**10**
0	0	0	0	0	0	0	0	0	0	0	0	0	0	0	0	0	0	0	0	0	0	0	0	0	0	0	0	**9**
0	X	0	0	0	X	0	0	0	X	0	0	0	X	0	0	0	X	0	0	0	X	0	0	0	X	0	0	**8**
X	X	X	0	X	X	X	0	X	X	X	0	X	X	X	0	X	X	X	0	X	X	X	0	X	X	X	0	**7**
X	X	X	X	X	X	X	X	X	X	X	X	X	X	X	X	X	X	X	X	X	X	X	X	X	X	X	X	**6**
X	/	X	X	X	/	X	X	X	/	X	X	X	/	X	X	X	/	X	X	X	/	X	X	X	/	X	X	**5**
/	/	/	X	/	/	/	X	/	/	/	X	/	/	/	X	/	/	/	X	/	/	/	X	/	/	/	X	**4**
/	/	/	/	/	/	/	/	/	/	/	/	/	/	/	/	/	/	/	/	/	/	/	/	/	/	/	/	**3**
/	-	/	/	/	-	/	/	/	-	/	/	/	-	/	/	/	-	/	/	/	-	/	/	/	-	/	/	**2**
-	-	-	/	-	-	-	/	-	-	-	/	-	-	-	/	-	-	-	/	-	-	-	/	-	-	-	/	**1**

Luskentyre chart.

Method

Front

Using 3.75mm needles and pale blue, cast on 100 sts, and work 2 rows st st.

Follow the Argyll chart, using the following colour sequence:

* Work 6 rows with pale blue and X = cream.
Work 6 rows with grey and X = cream.
Work 6 rows with grey and X = charcoal.
Work 6 rows with pale blue and X = charcoal.
Work 2 rows st st with pale blue.
Work 2 rows st st with grey.

Follow the Luskentyre chart, using the accompanying colour key, until all of the chart rows have been worked.

□ cream
- grey
/ sea blue
X bright blue
0 pale blue
\ charcoal

Colour key for the Luskentyre chart.

Work 2 rows st st with grey, and rep from * once.
Repeat the Argyll chart with the established colour sequence over 24 rows, then work 2 rows st st with pale blue.

Back

Continue by working the back of the cushion cover, which is knitted by following the Argyll chart only, with alternate yarn colours changing every 12 rows.

Note that the background colours become the foreground colours elsewhere within the pattern, which adds to the interest of the design and creates surprises.

Follow the Argyll chart throughout, using the following colour sequence:

Work 6 rows with grey and X = cream.
Work 6 rows with sea blue and X = cream.
Work 6 rows with sea blue and X = pale blue.
Work 6 rows with charcoal and X = pale blue.
Work 6 rows with charcoal and X = cream.
Work 6 rows with grey and X = cream.
Work 6 rows with grey and X = sea blue.
Work 6 rows with pale blue and X = sea blue.
Work 6 rows with pale blue and X = charcoal.
Work 6 rows with cream and X = charcoal.
Work 6 rows with cream and X = grey.
Work 6 rows with sea blue and X = grey.
Work 6 rows with sea blue and X = pale blue, and so on.

Design your own

Photocopy the Fair Isle 1 chart and, adding shading with colouring pencils, which can be rubbed out if the wrong colour is used, try out various colour combinations. It is much easier to use a coloured chart than a symbols-only chart.

To design your own colourways, use colouring pencils and photocopies of existing black-and-white charts.

Luskentyre beach.

Follow the Argyll chart until 152 rows have been worked (the back will now be the same length as the front).

Cast off loosely.

Finishing and making up

Sew in all yarn tails, trim the ends and wash, block and steam-press the fabric.

Fold the cushion cover in half (the fold line will be between the top of the front and start of the all-over Argyll pattern of the back). With a length of one of the yarn colours, sew together the LH edges and the RH edges to form side seams, then sew in and trim the seaming-yarn ends.

Insert the cushion pad, and either sew the entire bottom opening closed with a length of yarn or, if desired, sew in a zip with sewing thread.

Over-sew the top fold line of the cushion, to produce a fake seam, if desired.

Garden texture

Plaited garden-bench pillow

The plaited cable has the appearance of being complicated; it is in fact quite easy. The results are a thick and crunchy textured fabric, which looks like plaited rope standing proud from the background stitches.

The finished pillow has stitched highlights between the cables and also running through the cables. The subtle contrast of the almond-coloured yarn adds to the visual interest and gives the plait more visual depth.

Size
To fit a cushion pad, 62cm × 42cm (24½in × 16½in)

Yarn
Rowan Felted Tweed Aran – 8 × 50g balls of 765 Scree
Rowan Pure Wool Worsted – 1 × 100g ball 103 Almond, for optional embellishment

Needles
A pair of 4mm (US6, UK8) straight needles
A 3mm (US2–3, UK11) dpn, for cabling (this size is smaller than that recommended on the ball band, because a tight, firm fabric is required)

Extras
Optional zip, 36cm (14in)

Tension
27 sts and 27 rows = 10cm (4in) over the plait-cable stitch pattern, after washing and a light pressing

Plaited garden-bench pillow.

Detail showing the running-stitch embellishment of the plaited garden-bench pillow.

Plait-cable stitch pattern

For definitions of the knitting-term abbreviations used in this pattern, and later on in the book, see the section 'Abbreviations' in Chapter 1.

Worked over 13 sts.
Row 1 (RS) P2, k9, p2.
Row 2 K2, p9, k2.
Row 3 P2, sl the next 3 sts to the dpn and hold at the front of work, k3, k3 from the dpn, k3, p2.
Rows 4 and 6 Rep row 2.
Row 5 Rep row 1.
Row 7 P2, k3, sl the next 3 sts to the dpn and hold at the back of work, k3, k3 from the dpn, p2.
Row 8 Rep row 2.
Rep rows 1–8.

Method

Using 4mm needles and Scree, cast on 78 sts, and work six adjacent repeats of the cable by following the instructions for the plait-cable stitch pattern.

Continue as established until the fabric measures 122cm (48½in), and cast off.

Finishing and making up

Sew in all yarn tails, trim the ends and wash, block and lightly press the fabric.

Fold the fabric in half so that the short ends meet. Sew together the LH edges and the RH edges to form side seams.

Insert the cushion pad, and work the finishing embellishment if desired. It is much easier to do this with the cushion placed inside the cover, and this helps to prevent pulling the sewn stitches too tightly.

Thread a tapestry needle with Almond, and work a running stitch under and over the ridges made by one column of purl stitches between the cables.

Repeat this step for an adjacent column of purl stitches, offsetting the stitches that are worked under and over for this second row of running stitch.

Again using a tapestry needle threaded with Almond, weave the thread through the centre of each cable, taking the needle under every cable crossing. Do not pull the thread tightly, because the yarn will disappear and distort the cable.

Either sew the entire bottom opening closed with a length of yarn or, if desired, sew in a zip with sewing thread.

Design your own

When knitting a plaited cable, the stitches should be divisible by three, and the middle group of stitches is worked on every cabled row, first to the right, held at the front, and then to the left, held at the back. Larger plaits are very effective and can be made up of nine, twelve or fifteen stitches, and so on; however, extra rows should be added between the cable crossings to keep the proportion of the plait correct. Experiment to see which numbers of stitches and rows work best.

CHAPTER 4

THROWS AND BLANKETS

All of the blankets and throws in this chapter are worked with yarns that are made of wool or wool mixtures. Whether these furnishings are worked with chunky cables or finer four-ply yarn for Fair Isle patterns, there is no doubt that in your home they will create a great sensual effect. The wonderful colours and textures of the completed projects will help to counteract some of the harsh sensory effects of the world today. A blanket or throw draped over the bed will not only keep you warm but also give psychological comfort. In addition, there is evidence to suggest that babies sleep better when in contact with a lightweight wool.

The following examples of throws and blankets can be a catalyst for many other designs and colourways.

The colours used when designing the blankets and throws are informed by all that is absorbed from walks, reading, art exhibitions and nature. The knitted piece is treated as a canvas, and the threads are the paint. Walk in the woods or along a coastal path, and observe the transformation of a scene by the elements, the sun, wind and rain, which constantly change the shades of the colours around you. Observe the layering of clouds and the sky meeting the horizon, which one moment is a straight line and then a haze disappearing into

RIGHT: A selection of throws.

OPPOSITE: Throws and blankets.

Throws and blankets in a wood.

Play around with colours from your stash. Every knitter has a stash: bags of wonderful, odd balls of yarn. Choose an odd number of colours to work with; for example, five, perhaps yellow, green, pink, blue and purple. Work only in stripes of an even number of rows; these stripes are a neutral vehicle that will allow the colours to breathe and be seen without pattern complication. Each of these colours will change in its characteristics, depending on the colours that it is placed next to. Add colours, take other colours out and do the hokey-cokey with yarn!

Depth and density can be achieved by adding earth colours, such as brick red, plum, grey, stone, olive green and peat brown, and, when working a Fair Isle pattern, juxtapose neon lime green, acid yellow and pillar-box red: the result will be vibrant and exciting and a real feast for the beholder.

Be open to taking advantage of what occurs when certain colours are placed next to each other: embrace the accidental. The most challenging exercise is trying to recover what an event or experience was like at the time and represent it through the medium of yarn, by texture, stitch and colour.

A damp wood in the highlands, with gnarled old trees, and many clearings, provided a lovely setting to show off the Aran-patchwork blanket and Fair Isle and braid throws.

a storm. Study the sea; the vitality of the waves, the colours darting and skipping, busily jumping around: they are bright, colourful and lively, but with a rhythm of blue, green and shades in between. In your designs, try to highlight shades with a dark or light colour placed to create a pause, as this will enhance the viewer's overall perception of the piece.

Tweed effect

Tweedy throw

A wonderful, colourful, warm, cosy throw, knitted with myriad colours from the Rowan Felted Tweed range. Slip stitches and colour changes make this a versatile woven fabric that can be changed by using a different colour palette.

Size
Length × width, 193cm × 86cm (76in × 34in)

Yarn
Rowan Felted Tweed – 1 × 50g ball each of 183 Peony (A), 196 Red Barn (B), 185 Frozen (C), 145 Treacle (D), 154 Ginger (E), 158 Pine (F), 191 Granite (G), 181 Mineral (H), 152 Watery (I), 186 Tawny (J), 194 Delft (K), 150 Rage (L) and 151 Bilberry (M)

Needles
A pair of 4.5mm (US7, UK7) straight needles

Tension
21 sts and 30 rows = 10cm (4in) over the tweedy-throw stitch pattern, after washing and pressing

Note
· When changing yarn colours, weave the yarn tails in along the row while knitting, to keep the work neat.

Tweedy throw.

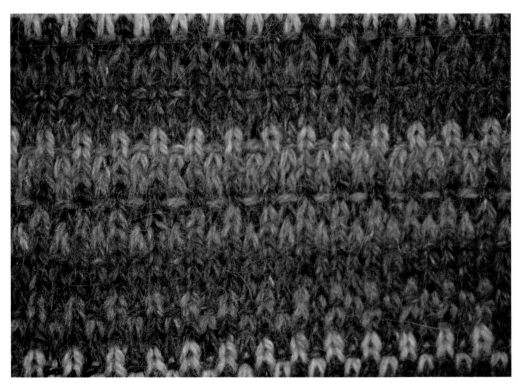

Stitch detail of the tweedy throw.

Tweedy-throw stitch pattern

Worked over an odd number of stitches.

Row 1 (RS) K1, * sl 1 st wyif, k1; rep from * to end.
Row 2 P across.
Row 3 K1, * sl 1 st wyib, k1; rep from * to end.
Row 4 P across.
Rep rows 1–4.

Method

Using 4.5mm needles and A, cast on 99 sts.
Work rows 1–4 of the tweedy-throw stitch pattern throughout, following the colour-change sequence below:

Row 1 (RS) With B, k1, * sl 1 st wyif, k1; rep from * to end.
Row 2 With B, p across.
Row 3 With C, k1, * sl 1 st wyib, k1; rep from * to end.
Row 4 With C, p across.
Row 5 With D, k1, * sl 1 st wyif, k1; rep from * to end.
Row 6 With D, p across.
Row 7 With E, rep row 3.
Row 8 With E, rep row 4.
Row 9 With F, rep row 1.
Row 10 With F, rep row 2.
Row 11 With G, rep row 3.
Row 12 With G, rep row 4.
Row 13 With H, rep row 1.
Row 14 With H, rep row 2.

Design your own

Try out colourways by wrapping the yarns around a card or knitting small swatches and sewing them together for a cushion. Pick all the dark colours or bright colours that you can find, and see how they look together.

Row 15 With I, rep row 3.
Row 16 With I, rep row 4.
Row 17 With J, rep row 1.
Row 18 With J, rep row 2.
Row 19 With K, rep row 3.
Row 20 With K, rep row 4.
Row 21 With L, rep row 1.
Row 22 With L, rep row 2.
Row 23 With M, rep row 3.
Row 24 With M, rep row 4.
Repeat the colour sequence until the fabric measures 193cm (76in) or the yarn has been used up!
Cast off in pattern.

Finishing

Sew in all yarn tails, if you did not weave them in while knitting, and trim the ends.
 Wash, block and press the throw.

Pixel blanket in the garden.

Pixels and hearts

Pixel blanket

Strip knitting is a wonderful way to make exciting colour combinations, and it breaks down larger projects, so they are easily transportable. Although the starburst effect is based on more traditional quilt patterns, the colours are inspired by a pixilated pencil drawing that was enlarged on a screen to such a magnification that the drawn lines became pixilated. The colours that this treatment revealed became the creative inspiration for this blanket.

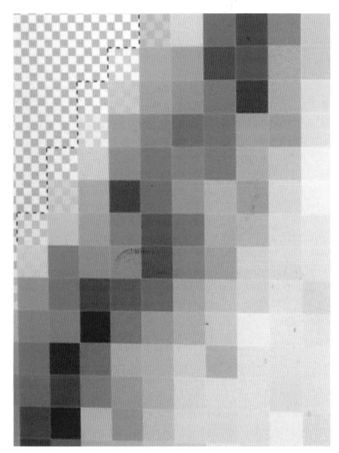

Pixel inspiration.

The strips are worked with stocking stitch, with different colours being joined in to work adjacent blocks of colour. When the strips are sewn together, they produce an effective, bright and colourful patchwork.

Size
Length × width, 160cm × 145cm (63in × 57in)

Yarn
Rowan Felted Tweed – 2 × 50g balls each of 197 Alabaster (A), 191 Granite (B), 175 Cumin (C), 170 Seafarer (D), 151 Bilberry (E), 192 Amethyst (F), 167 Maritime (G), 178 Seasalter (H), 194 Delft (I), 177 Clay (J), 186 Tawny (K) and 157 Camel (L), for knitting the blanket, and 1 x 50g ball of 183 Peony, for the optional crocheted edging

Needles
A pair of 4mm (US6, UK8) straight needles
A 3mm (US2–3, UK11) crochet hook, for the optional crocheted-edging embellishment

Tension
22 sts and 30 rows = 10cm (4in) over st st, after washing and pressing

Method
Using 4mm needles and H, cast on 22 sts, and work 30 rows, to complete the first colour block.

Change to L, and work 30 rows, to complete the second colour block.

Follow the 17-block colour-change sequence shown in the accompanying chart until the first strip has been completed.

Cast off loosely.

Complete all fifteen strips.

Making up
Block and press all of the strips, then sew them together in the correct order with mattress stitch.

Sew in all yarn tails, and trim the ends.

							Strip No									
		1	2	3	4	5	6	7	8	9	10	11	12	13	14	15
	17	H	C	E	D	C	F	K	C	E	F	C	D	E	C	H
	16	L	H	D	C	F	E	C	H	C	E	F	C	D	H	L
	15	E	D	C	F	E	G	B	C	B	G	E	F	C	D	E
	14	D	C	F	E	G	B	H	K	H	B	G	E	F	C	D
	13	L	F	E	G	B	H	I	J	I	H	B	G	E	F	L
	12	F	E	G	B	H	K	A	D	A	K	H	B	G	E	F
	11	E	G	B	H	G	J	D	A	D	J	G	H	B	G	E
	10	L	B	H	E	J	D	A	F	A	D	J	E	H	B	L
Block No	9	H	C	G	J	D	J	F	L	F	J	D	J	G	C	H
	8	L	B	H	E	J	D	A	F	A	D	J	E	H	B	L
	7	E	G	B	H	G	J	D	A	D	J	G	H	B	G	E
	6	F	E	G	B	H	K	A	D	A	K	H	B	G	E	F
	5	L	F	E	G	B	H	I	A	I	H	B	G	E	F	L
	4	D	C	F	E	G	B	H	E	H	B	G	E	F	C	D
	3	E	D	C	F	E	G	B	C	B	G	E	F	C	D	E
	2	L	H	D	C	F	E	C	H	C	E	F	C	D	H	L
	1	H	C	E	D	C	F	K	C	E	F	C	D	E	C	H

Colour-change-sequence chart for the pixel blanket.

Detail of the pixel blanket.

Detail of the crocheted edging of the pixel blanket.

Finishing

Using a 3mm crochet hook and Peony, work a double-crochet edging (*see* Appendix for instructions to work this embellishment) around the entire perimeter of the blanket.

Insert the hook 1 row in from the cast-on and cast-off edges at the bottom and top of the blanket, respectively, and 1 st away from the LH and RH edges of the blanket.

Work into 1 st and skip the next st (in other words, work into every other st along the perimeter). Work 3 extra, adjacent sts at each corner, so the edging will lie flat.

Using Delft (I), in the same manner, work a second row of double-crochet edging.

Sew in and trim all remaining yarn tails, and wash, block and lightly press the blanket.

Hearts cot cover

This cot cover is a perfect project for using up odd balls of yarn, and it is made in the same way as the pixel blanket.

Eleven colours were used for this cover, but the colours can be pared down if required, and each block contains a heart embellishment of a contrasting colour. The colours chosen for this cover are fairly random; however, they would suit any baby.

Each of the seven strips contains seven blocks that are 11cm (4¼in) square. The approximate weight of 300g of four-ply yarn is required for a completed cover.

Size
77cm (30½in) square

Yarn
Four-ply yarn – approximately 300g in total

Needles
A pair of 3.75mm (US5, UK9) straight needles

Hearts cot cover.

H	D	G	H	G	D	H
A	K	I	J	I	K	A
F	A	B	A	B	A	F
I	K	E	J	E	K	I
F	A	C	A	B	A	F
A	K	I	J	I	K	A
J	D	G	C	G	D	J

Colour-key chart for the hearts cot cover.

Tension

33 sts and 24.5 rows = 10cm (4in) over st st, after washing and pressing

Method

To produce the pattern of the cover, either knit in the hearts using the intarsia technique or Swiss darn them after the cover has been knitted; whichever method is used to work the hearts, select a yarn colour that contrasts with the yarn colour of the block.

Follow the method for the pixel blanket and the accompanying heart chart, and experiment with placement of the hearts within the blocks; perhaps try placing some heats off-centre, to see whether you like the effect.

	X	X				X	X	
X	X	X	X		X	X	X	X
X	X	X	X	X	X	X	X	X
X	X	X	X	X	X	X	X	X
	X	X	X	X	X	X	X	
		X	X	X	X	X		
			X	X	X			
				X				

Swiss-darning or intarsia heart chart for the hearts cot cover.

Making up

Block and press all of the strips, then sew them together in the correct order with mattress stitch.
Sew in all yarn tails, and trim the ends.

Finishing

The cot cover can be finished by blanket stitching around the edges with a contrasting colour of yarn (*see* Appendix for instructions to work this embellishment).

Sudoko throws

This is a fun project, with almost endless colour variations being possible.

While wandering around the Tate Gallery one day, I picked up a card of a hand-coloured etching entitled Colour Sudoku by artist Tom Phillips. Each square was divided into nine and then again into nine, with no colour repeating in each square or line up or down. This fitted in well with the strip-knitting technique and was the catalyst for this project.

The sudoku throws are made in the same way as the pixel blanket, with the autumn-throw and summer-border-throw examples being made up of 9cm (3½in) squares of 22 sts × 30 rows.

Yarn-colour clippings for the sudoku throws.

Size
Length × width, 81cm (32in) × 81cm (32in)

Yarn
Four-ply, wool yarn – approximately 300g in total

Needles
A pair of 3.75mm (US5, UK9) straight needles

Tension
24.5 sts x 33 rows = 10cm (4in) over st st, after washing and pressing

Autumn throw

Nine shades of oranges, browns, greens, beiges and yellow were chosen to capture the essence of autumn in this throw, with an edging of green, falling leaves.

Method
Follow the method for the pixel blanket. Work the nine strips required, following the accompanying colour-key chart, and sew them together with mattress stitch,

D	A	F	I	G	H	C	B	E
G	C	B	E	A	D	F	I	H
I	H	E	B	F	C	A	G	D
B	E	D	C	I	A	H	F	G
H	G	A	F	E	B	I	D	C
F	I	C	H	D	G	E	A	B
A	D	I	G	C	E	B	H	F
E	F	H	D	B	I	G	C	A
C	B	G	A	H	F	D	E	I

Colour-key chart for the sudoku throws.

Autumn throw.

Detail of the falling-leaf edging.

Worked over 8 sts.

Cast on 8 sts.

Row 1 (RS) K5, yo, k1, yo, k2.
Row 2 P6, kfb, k3.
Row 3 K4, p1, k2, yo, k1, yo, k3.
Row 4 P8, kfb, k4.
Row 5 K4, p2, k3, yo, k1, yo, k4.
Row 6 P10, kfb, k5.
Row 7 K4, p3, k4, yo, k1, yo, k5.
Row 8 P12, kfb, k6.
Row 9 K4, p4, ssk, k7, k2tog, k1.
Row 10 P10, kfb, k7.
Row 11 K4, p5, ssk, k5, k2tog, k1.
Row 12 P8, kfb, k2, p1, k5.
Row 13 K4, p1, k1, p4, ssk, k3, k2tog, k1.
Row 14 P6, kfb, k3, p1, k5.
Row 15 K4, p1, k1, p5, ssk, k1, k2tog, k1.
Row 16 P4, kfb, k4, p1, k5.
Row 17 K4, p1, k1, p6, sl1–k2tog–psso, k1.
Row 18 P2tog, cast off the next 5 sts by using p2tog to cast off the first st, p3, k4.

Rep rows 1–18 for the desired length of the edging, ending at the completion of a leaf.

Cast off.

Finishing

Stitch the edging in place to the perimeter of the throw, taking care to ease the edging around the corners, so that the edging will lie flat.

Neatly stitch together the cast-on and cast-off ends of the edging.

Sew in all yarn tails, and trim the ends.

Wash, block and press the throw.

ensuring that they are correctly arranged. It is a good idea to label each strip when it is being worked.

Finish with a separately knitted falling-leaf edging that is sewn to the perimeter of the throw.

Falling-leaf edging
Abbreviation:
kfb – knit into the front of the next stitch on the LH needle, do not remove the stitch knitted into (the original stitch) from the LH needle, knit into the back of the original stitch, then allow the original stitch to drop from the LH needle (a one-stitch increase).

Summer-border throw

Bright primary colours were used for this throw. A cheery summer border, with geraniums, nasturtiums, petunias and lupins, rising like sky rockets, was the catalyst for this design.

Method
Follow the instructions for the autumn throw. The

Summer-border throw.

throw is edged with Diane's-border edging, a pretty lace zigzag worked with a primary colour, red.

Diane's-border edging
Worked over 5 sts.
Cast on 5 sts.
Row 1 K2, yo, k2tog, yo, k1.
Row 2 K across.
Row 3 K3, yo, k2tog, yo, k1.
Row 4 K across.
Row 5 K4, yo, k2tog, yo, k1.
Row 6 K across.
Row 7 K5, yo, k2tog, yo, k1.
Rows 8 and 9 K across.
Row 10 Cast off 4 sts, k to end.
Rep rows 1–10 until the edging is long enough to be placed around the perimeter of the throw, and cast off.

Finishing
Finish as for the autumn throw.

Design your own

Choose nine colours from whatever inspiration you are using or at random! Decide how large you require the cot cover, sofa throw, picnic blanket or bed cover to be. Knit a tension swatch, and work out how big the squares need to be to fit into the finished item nine times. If an oblong shape is required, for example, for a cot blanket, add a few extra rows to each square.

Allocate each colour a letter, and work nine strips of the coloured squares. For the arrangement of the coloured squares, see the accompanying sudoku-throws colour-key chart.

Include one of the edgings shown on the sample throws, or substitute any edging that you think will complement your design, using the edgings featured throughout this book for inspiration.

Bauhaus blanket and throw

Bauhaus blanket

My aim with this project was to use a few subtle colours and make a large blanket for a double bed.

I have studied the Bauhaus period in design history and was impressed with the variety that had been achieved with a limited colour palette and blocks of colour being interrupted with stripes.

As this was to be a large project, it needed to be made smaller for it to be possible to carry around and knit, so strip knitting was the answer. This method makes a large item easier to handle and not so weighty when knitting it up.

Planning on paper is essential, in order to know which colours are to go where and what size the colour blocks and strips need to be. I knitted a tension swatch and ascertained that I needed twelve strips of 100 sts to obtain the intended width and nine 100-row blocks of colour for the intended length. Each block needed to be 20cm (8in) wide and 25.5cm (10in) long.

Size

Length × width, approximately 240cm × 229.5cm (94½in × 90½in)

Yarn

Knoll Yarns Soft Donegal, 100 per cent pure-merino wool (but any four-ply yarn can be used) – 10 × 50g balls each of 5511 Unshin (charcoal, A), 5507 Swilly (cream, B), 5529 Eske (grey, C) and 5518 Boyne (beige, E) and 15 × 50g of 5519 Moy (pale blue, D)

Remember that, if you intend to felt your blanket, a wool yarn or a wool-mixture yarn must be used.

Needles

A pair of 2.75mm (US1, UK13) straight needles
A 3mm (US2–3, UK11) crochet hook

Tension

26 sts and 42 rows = 10cm (4in) over st st, after washing and pressing

Method

Using 2.75mm needles, cast on 100 sts, and work the 100-row blocks for each of the twelve strips, as indicated in the accompanying colour-change-sequence chart.

Some blocks are worked with a single colour, while others, with two colours indicated, are worked with alternate-colour 10-row stripes, starting with the colour indicated by the first letter.

Add a marker to the end of each strip, as this will help you achieve the correct stripe arrangement when sewing up.

Making up

Sew the first two strips together with mattress stitch, using the markers to help you to identify each block. Join each remaining strip to the blanket in the correct order.

Bauhaus blanket.

Colour-change-sequence chart for the Bauhaus blanket.

		Strip No											
		1	2	3	4	5	6	7	8	9	10	11	12
	9	C	E/B	E/D	D	D/B	B	A/B	A/B	C/D	B	A/B	A/B
	8	B/A	A	E	B/D	D	D/C	B	A	C	B/D	A	D
	7	D/B	E/B	D	E/B	B	A/D	B/D	B	C/D	A/D	B	A/C
	6	D	A	A/B	E	E/D	A	C	B/E	E	A	D/C	D
Block No	5	D	A/B	A/B	B	E/D	B	D/C	E/B	E/D	C	D/C	D/C
	4	D/E	D	D	B/A	A	B/E	E	D	A	C/D	E	E
	3	D/C	D	E/D	C/D	D/C	A/C	B	A/B	C	A/B	A/B	B
	2	A	D/E	E	D	E	D	B/A	A	C/D	E	A	B/A
	1	A/B	C	C/D	C/D	A/B	C/D	D	C/D	B	E/D	E/D	D

Sew in all yarn tails, and trim the ends.

When the blanket is complete, you can then decide whether you want to felt it.

Felting will make a more dense fabric and result in a blanket that is smaller in size. Use the washing-machine method, at 40°C, with an 800rpm spin cycle. For some additional guidance, *see* the notes about felting with a washing machine in the section 'Felting' in Chapter 2.

If your washing-machine interface or manual does not have details about temperature, rpm and washing times, you will have to knit a test piece and use trial and error to determine how the felting process occurs with different settings and to decide how dense you require the felted fabric to be.

Finishing

Using a 3mm crochet hook and Swilly (cream), inserting the hook 3 rows in or 3 sts away from the edge of the blanket and into 3 sts out of every 4 sts, work 2 rows of double-crochet edging (*see* Appendix for instructions to work this embellishment) around the entire perimeter of the blanket. Work 3 extra, adjacent sts at each corner, so the edging will lie flat.

Sew in and trim all remaining yarn tails, and wash, block and lightly press the blanket.

Nautical Bauhaus throw

It is all in the scale: this is the same pattern as for the Bauhaus blanket but scaled down (however, this version is not felted). Bright blue and yellow are colours that work well together. The grey and pale blue contrasting shades allow the yellow and blue colours to breathe, and they seem brighter for it.

The nautical feel of this throw has been enhanced by the addition of a knitted edging called shark's tooth; this edging also looks like waves or pennants on the rigging of boats.

Bauhaus blanket at a larger size before felting.

Nautical Bauhaus throw in the garden.

Choose your own colours, and alter the number of striped rows and of colour blocks for a completely different look.

Size
Width × length, approximately 86cm × 140cm (34in × 55in)

Yarn
Knoll Yarns Soft Donegal, 100 per cent pure-merino wool (or any four-ply yarn that knits up to the required tension) – 3 × 50g each of 5527 Roe (bright blue, A), 5571 Hickory (yellow, B), 5508 Foyle (beige, C), 5580 Silver Mist (grey, D) and 5548 Malone (pale blue, E)

Needles
A pair of 2.25mm (US1, UK13) straight needles

Tension
26 sts and 40 rows = 10cm (4in) over st st, after washing and pressing

Method
Using 2.25mm needles, follow the colour-change-sequence chart and instructions for the larger version of this Bauhaus pattern, but each strip has a width of 30 sts and the blocks are each worked over 40 rows, so the striped blocks feature 4-row stripes.

Mark the end of each block, because this will help you to achieve the correct block arrangement when sewing up.

When all of the strips have been completed, sew them together with mattress stitch, matching the marked blocks.

While the edging is optional, it really does make a difference and finishes the throw beautifully.

Shark's-tooth edging
Worked throughout using A, B and E only.
Using A, cast on 8 sts, and knit 1 row.
Row 1 Sl 1 st, k1,(yo, k2tog) twice, yo, k2.
Row 2 K2, yo, k2, (yo, k2tog) twice, k1.
Row 3 Sl 1 st, k1, (yo, k2tog) twice, k2, yo, k2.
Row 4 K2, yo, k4, (yo, k2tog) twice, k1.
Row 5 Sl 1 st, k1, (yo, k2tog) twice, k4, yo, k2.
Row 6 K2, yo, k6, (yo, k2tog) twice, k1.
Row 7 Sl 1 st, k1, (yo, k2tog) twice, k6, yo, k2.
Row 8 K2, yo, k8, (yo, k2tog) twice, k1.
Row 9 Sl 1 st, k1, (yo, k2tog) twice, k8, yo, k2.
Row 10 K2, yo, k10, (yo, k2tog) twice, k1.
Row 11 Sl 1 st, k1, (yo, k2tog) twice, k10, yo, k2.
Row 12 Cast off 11 sts, k2, (yo, k2tog) twice, k1.
Change to B, and rep rows 1–12.
Change to E, and rep rows 1–12.

Continue as established until there is enough edging to be sewn in place around the entire perimeter of the throw, ending with a completed pattern repeat (a full tooth worked with E).
Cast off.

Finishing
Stitch the edging in place to the perimeter of the throw, taking care to ease the edging around the corners, so that the edging will lie flat.

Neatly stitch together the cast-on and cast-off edges of the edging.

Sew in all yarn tails, and trim the ends.

Wash, block and press the throw.

Fair Isle

Fair Isle patterns are versatile and have a unique appeal. One chart can be used in many different ways, by alter-

ing the colours to create a different style. Fair Isle can be used in stripes or as all-over patterns, offering great flexibility to design throws and blankets.

Fair Isle throw

In the patches of this throw, smaller stripes worked with a single contrast-colour yarn surround a larger, multicoloured stripe.

Nautical Bauhaus throw on display.

Fair Isle throw.

Three Fair Isle patches featuring contrasting colourways are worked and pieced together into a patchwork throw.

Patch A uses shades of blue and lilac, the inspiration being the Hebridean sea and surf just off the coast of Harris.

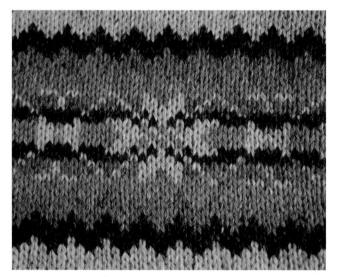

Knitted sample with the patch A colourway of the Fair Isle 1 chart.

Patch B features the colours of the heathery hillsides and clumps of different grasses being grazed by cattle and sheep in a Scottish landscape.

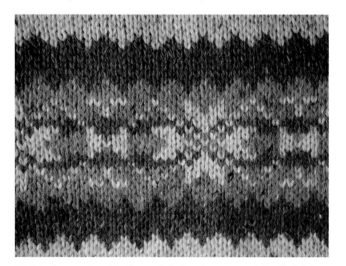

Knitted sample with the patch B colourway of the Fair Isle 1 chart.

Patch C corresponds to the deep, dark, peaty burn water that crashes down in a waterfall and over the rocks at Blair Atholl.

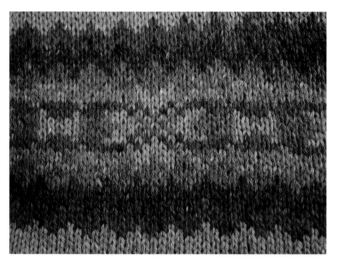

Knitted sample with the patch C colourway of the Fair Isle 1 chart.

The Fair Isle 1 and Fair Isle 2 charts are used for this Fair Isle throw: see the section 'Fair Isle cushions' in Chapter 3.

Size
Width × length, 113cm × 155cm (44in × 60½in)
Each patch measures 24cm × 28cm (9½in × 11in)

Yarn
Rowan Felted Tweed – 2 × 50g balls each of 194 Delft, 157 Camel, 177 Clay, 152 Watery, 197 Alabaster and 167 Maritime and 1 × 50g ball each of 154 Ginger, 175 Cinnamon, 196 Red Barn, 186 Tawny, 151 Bilberry, 183 Peony, 191 Granite, 170 Seafarer and 192 Amethyst

Needles
A pair of 3.75mm (US5, UK9) straight needles
A 3mm (US2–3, UK11) crochet hook
Change needle size as necessary to obtain the correct tension.

Tension

23 sts and 30 rows = 10cm (4in) over st st, after washing and pressing

Note

- Read the charts from right to left on RS row and left to right on WS rows.
- When working in pattern, use the Fair Isle technique, by stranding yarn not in use loosely across the back of the work.
- When changing yarn colours, weave in the yarn tails while knitting.

Method

Patch A

Make eight patches.

Using 3.75mm needles and Alabaster, cast on 54 sts.

Work 6 rows st st.

Work the Fair Isle 2 chart with - = Alabaster and X = Amethyst.

Work 6 rows st st with Alabaster.

Work the Fair Isle 1 chart, following the accompanying colour key.

-	Alabaster (A)
/	Seafarer (B)
X	Granite (C)
0	Maritime (D)
\	Amethyst (E)

Colour key for patch A of the Fair Isle throw.

Work 6 rows st st with Alabaster.

Work the Fair Isle 2 chart with - = Alabaster and X = Seafarer.

Work 6 rows st st with Alabaster, and cast off.

Patch B

Make eight patches.

Using 3.75mm needles and Clay, cast on 54 sts.

* Work 6 rows st st.

Work the Fair Isle 2 chart with - = Clay and X = Watery.

Work 6 rows st st with Clay *.

Work Fair Isle 1 chart, following the accompanying colour key.

Rep from * to * once, and cast off.

-	Clay (A)
/	Bilberry (B)
X	Tawny (C)
0	Peony (D)
\	Watery (E)

Colour key for patch B of the Fair Isle throw.

Patch C

Make nine patches.

Using 3.75mm needles and Camel, cast on 54 sts.

* Work 6 rows st st.

Work the Fair Isle 2 chart with - = Camel and X = Delft.

Work 6 rows st st with Camel *.

Work the Fair Isle 1 chart, following the accompanying colour key.

-	Camel (A)
/	Ginger (B)
X	Red Barn (C)
0	Cinnamon (D)
\	Delft (E)

Colour key for patch C of the Fair Isle throw.

Rep from * to * once, and cast off.

Making up

Using the accompanying assembly diagram, sew the A, B and C patches together to form an oblong that is five patches wide and five patches long.

Strip No				
1	2	3	4	5
B	C	A	B	C
C	A	B	C	A
A	B	C	A	B
B	C	A	B	C
C	A	B	C	A

Assembly diagram for the Fair Isle throw.

Finishing

Using a 3mm crochet hook, work a double-crochet edging (*see* Appendix for instructions to work this embellishment) around the entire perimeter of the throw.

Work 3 rows in total, working 1 row each with the contrasting colours Peony, Delft and Ginger.

Insert the hook 1 row in or 1 st away from the edge of the throw, and work into 3 sts out of every 4 sts. Work 3 extra, adjacent sts at each corner, so the edging will lie flat.

Wash, block and press the throw.

Texture and lace

Aran-patchwork blanket

This delightful, crunchy cabled blanket is well worth the effort to knit with an aran-weight, pure-wool yarn. It is knitted as five strips that are sewn together to make a patchwork featuring seven different blocks of cables and stitch patterns.

Design your own

To make a blanket, simply add extra patches to achieve the width and length that you require.

Size
Width × length, 150cm × 153cm (59in × 60in)

Yarn
Knoll Yarns Soft Donegal, NM 8/2 100 per cent pure merino wool – 30 × 50g balls of 5307 Swilly

Needles
A pair of 7mm (US10–11, UK2) straight needles
A 6mm (US10, UK4) dpn, for cabling (using a dpn that is one size smaller than the main needle used for knitting the pattern makes for a tighter cable)

The Fair Isle throw, among the granite rocks and heathery wild flowers that supplied the inspiration for this project.

Aran-patchwork blanket.

Tension
40 sts and 32 rows = 20cm (8in) over st st, after washing and a light pressing

Note
- Use sticky notes to mark where you are in the pattern, or use paper and pencil to keep track of your progress.

Method
Using 7mm needles, cast on 40 sts, and purl 4 rows.

Work a block of bramble stitch by following the instructions below:

Bramble stitch (A)
Row 1 (RS) P across.
Row 2 * (k1, p1, k1) all in the same st, p3tog; rep from * to end.
Row 3 P across.
Row 4 * P3tog, (k1, p1, k1) all in the same st; rep from * to end.
Rep rows 1–4 until the bramble-stitch block measures 20cm (8in) in length.
Purl 4 rows.
Continue to work the strip, by working a block of crossed-cable stitch following the instructions below:

Crossed-cable stitch (B)
Abbreviations:
3-st left cable – sl 2 sts to the dpn and hold at the front of the work, k1, k2 from dpn.
3-st right cable – sl 1 st to the dpn and hold at the back of the work, k2, k1 from dpn.

4-st right cable – sl 2 sts to the dpn and hold at the back of the work, k2, k2 from dpn.
M1 – make one stitch: insert the LH needle tip from the front of the work to the back, pick up the strand of yarn that runs between the stitch closest to the tip of LH needle and the stitch to its right (the stitch directly below the last stitch knitted by the RH needle). Knit into the back of this picked-up strand, by inserting the RH needle tip from right to left under this picked-up loop so that the tip comes out at the back of the loop (a one-stitch increase).
Row 1 (RS) P1, * p4, 4-st right cable, p5; rep from * to end.
Row 2 K1, * k4, p4, k5; rep from * to end.
Row 3 P1, * p3, 3-st right cable, 3-st left cable, p4; rep from * to end.
Row 4 K1, * k3, p6, k4; rep from * to end.
Row 5 P1, * p2, 3-st right cable, k2, 3-st left cable, p3; rep from * to end.
Row 6 K1, * k2, p8, k3; rep from * to end.
Row 7 P1, * p1, 3-st right cable, k4, 3-st left cable, p2; rep from * to end.
Row 8 K1, * k1, p10, k2; rep from * to end.

Rep rows 1–8 until the crossed-cable-stitch block measures 20cm (8in) in length.

Purl 3 rows, increasing by 4 sts by working an M1 4 times, spaced evenly across the last row only (44 sts).

Continue to work the strip, by working a block of Aran-honeycomb stitch following the instructions below:

Aran-honeycomb stitch (C)
Abbreviations:

C2B sl 2 sts cn hold at back of work, k2, k2 from cn.

C2F sl 2 sts cn hold at front of work, k2, k2 from cn.

Row 1 (WS) and all other WS rows P across.

Row 2 * C2B, C2F; rep from * to end.

Row 4 K across.

Row 6 * C2F, C2B; rep from * to end.

Row 8 K across.

Rep rows 1–8 until the Aran-honeycomb-stitch block measures 20cm (8in) in length.

Purl 3 rows.

Continue to work the strip, by working a block of serpentine-cable stitch by following the instructions below:

Serpentine-cable stitch (D)
Abbreviations:

FC or front cross – sl 2 st to cn, hold in front of work, p1, then 2 from cn.

BC or back cross – sl 1 st to cn, hold at back of work, k2, then p1 from cn.

Row 1 (WS) K2, p2, * k4, p4; rep from * to the last 8 sts, k4, p2, k2.

Row 2 P2, * 3-st FC, p2, 3-st BC; rep from * to the last 2 sts, p2.

Row 3 and all subsequent WS rows Knit all k sts and purl all p sts.

Row 4 P3, * 3-st FC, 3-st BC, p2; rep from * to the last st, p1.

Row 6 * P4, C2B; rep from * to the last 4 sts, p4.

Row 8 P3, * 3-st BC, 3-st FC, p2; rep from * to the last st, p1.

Row 10 Knit all k sts and purl all p sts.

Row 12 P3, * 3-st FC, 3-st BC, p2; rep from * to the last st, p1.

Row 14 * P4, C2B; rep from * to the last 4 sts, p4.

Row 16 P3, * 3-st BC, 3-st FC, p2; rep from * to the last st, p1.

Row 18 P2, * 3-st BC, p2, 3-st FC; rep from * to the last 2 sts, p2.

Row 20 P1, 3-st BC, * p4, C2F; rep from * to the last 8 sts, p4, 3-st FC, p1.

Row 22 3-st BC, p4, * 3-st BC, 3-st FC, p2; rep from * to the last 5 sts, p2, 3-st FC.

Row 24 Knit all k sts and purl all p sts.

Row 26 3-st FC, p4, * 3-st FC, 3-st BC, p2; rep from * to the last 5 sts, p2, 3-st BC.

Row 28 P1, 3-st FC, * p4, C2F; rep from * to the last 8 sts, p4, 3-st BC, p1.

Rep rows 1–28 until the serpentine-cable-stitch block measures 20cm (8in) in length.

Purl 3 rows, decreasing by 2 sts by working a k2tog twice, spaced evenly across the last row only (42 sts).

Continue to work the strip, by working a block of shadow-cable stitch following the instructions below:

Shadow-cable stitch (E)
Row 1 (WS) and all other WS rows P across.

Row 2 K across.

Row 4 K1, * C2B, k4; rep from * to last st, k1.

Row 6 K across.

Row 8 K1, * k4, C2F; rep from * to last st, k1.

Rep rows 1–8 until the shadow-cable-stitch block measures 20cm (8in) in length.

Purl 4 rows, decreasing by 2 sts by working a k2tog twice, spaced evenly across the last row only (40 sts).

Continue to work the strip, by working a block of basic-lattice stitch following the instructions below:

Basic-lattice stitch (F)
Abbreviations:

2-st BC – sl 1 st to the dpn and hold at the back of the work, k1, then p1 from the dpn.

2-st FC – sl 1 st to the dpn and hold at the front of the work, p1, then k1 from the dpn.

C1B – sl 1 st to the dpn and hold at the back of the work, k1, then k1 from the dpn.

C1F – sl 1 st to the dpn and hold at the front of the work, k1, then k1 from the dpn.

Row 1 (RS) P3, C1B, * p6, C1B; rep from * to the last 3 sts, p3.

Row 2 and all other WS rows Knit all k sts and purl all p sts.

Stitch-pattern-sequence chart for the Aran-patchwork blanket.

Row 3 P2, * 2-st BC, 2-st FC, p4; rep from * to the last 6 sts, 2-st BC, 2-st FC, p2.
Row 5 P1, * 2-st BC, p2, 2-st FC, p2; rep from * to the last 7 sts, 2-st BC, p2, 2-st FC, p1.
Row 7 * 2-st BC, p4, 2-st FC; rep from * to end.
Row 9 K1, * p6, C1F; rep from * to the last 7 sts, p6, k1.
Row 11 * 2-st FC, p4, 2-st BC; rep from * to end.
Row 13 P1,* 2-st FC, p2, 2-st BC, p2; rep from * to the last 7 sts, 2-st FC, p2, 2-st BC, p1.
Row 15 P2, * 2-st FC, 2-st BC, p4; rep from * to the last 6 sts, 2-st FC, 2-st BC, p2.
Row 16 Rep row 2.
Rep rows 1–16 until the basic-lattice-stitch block measures 20cm (8in) in length.
Purl 4 rows.
Repeat working a 20cm (8in) bramble-stitch block, purl 4 rows, and cast off.
Following the stitch-pattern-sequence chart and referring to the instructions for stitch patterns A–F, work the four other patterned strips (strips 2–5).

		Strip No				
		1	2	3	4	5
	7	A	B	C	D	E
	6	F	A	B	C	D
	5	E	F	A	B	C
Block No	4	D	E	F	A	B
	3	C	D	E	F	A
	2	B	C	D	E	F
	1	A	B	C	D	E

that the strips are in the correct order and that the purl rows that separate each stitch-pattern block match up and are neatly in alignment.

Making up
Sew together the strips with mattress stitch, ensuring

Finishing
Wash, block and lightly press the blanket.

Stitch details of the Aran-patchwork blanket.

Design your own

Cables are great fun to design with. There are quite literally hundreds of cable variations that can be worked and then sewn together in panels. Cables and cable-stitch patterns are ideal to make furnishing fabrics; for example, four cushions with four different designs.

Intricate or chunky and rolling or climbing cables can be closely packed together, forming an almost sculptural piece of work. This can be achieved by separately keeping track of the current row number of each cable, to avoid getting in a muddle.

Cables are intended to be used in vertical panels, whereas cable-stitch patterns are repeated and therefore produce all-over patterns. They can be adapted and used in panels of one repeat only or two adjacent repeats. Using the repeat stitch count at the top of the pattern, plus the edge stitches, if any, work out how many stitches are needed for the required panel. For example, if the stitch pattern requires 10 sts plus 3 sts for an edging, a single panel of 13 sts can be worked or a double version of 23 sts.

Most cable patterns feature knit stitches on a purl-stitch background. When the knit stitches are worked vertically, they tend to stand out from the purl stitches. When knitted horizontally, the purl stitches tend to stand out from the knit stitches.

This is vital information if you decide to design a patchwork blanket, which mixes cables and cable stitches that start on RS or WS rows. Producing your own design will enable you to really get to know the stitches involved.

Experimenting with and exploring these attributes of cables is great problem-solving practice, but it is vital groundwork to producing an original piece, and it can save a lot of time further on in the process of knitting your design.

Braid throw.

Braid throw

The choice of yarn for this textured throw was a tweedy, soft, duck-egg colour of an alpaca–wool-mix yarn that will fit in with any interior. Cables offset by lacy panels, openwork stitch patterns outlined by a line of k1, p1, k1 stitches and varying widths of the panels all combine to create interesting textures.

These are the four stitch patterns that are featured in this throw:

A Cabled-feather pattern is a variation on the famous feather-and-fan stitch, with a swaying cable juxtaposed with a lacy wave. Based on an old Shetland pattern, there are many variations and adaptations of this stitch. It produces a scalloped edging that makes for an interesting finished edge.

B Clustered-braid pattern is a more unusual cable. The weaving rope-like cables climbing up the throw are accentuated by the yarn being wrapped around the cables, which are not twisted together.

C Fancy-shell pattern is a delicate, small, openwork, twisted-stitch pattern that is ideal for framing the larger twin-leaf pattern. It adds variety to the panels and highlights the size of the other, larger stitch patterns. Also used as the edging stitch pattern, it encloses the throw.

D Twin-leaf pattern is an intricate lacy pattern travelling up the throw that includes texture and contrasting openwork, which in turn acts as a foil to the smaller fancy-shell pattern positioned on each side. Based on the traditional leaf pattern and leaning out from a central line, it is not unlike a tree-of-life pattern.

Stitch details of the braid throw.

Size
Length × width, 210cm × 100cm (82½in × 39in)

Yarn
Rowan Felted Tweed Aran – 20 × 50g balls of 173 Duck Egg

Needles
A pair of 5mm (US8, UK6) straight needles
A 4mm (US6, UK8) dpn, for cabling

Tension
16 sts and 23 rows = 10cm (4in) over st st, after washing and a light pressing

Note
· The four stitch patterns are worked in nine panels in a regularly repeating sequence across each row to make up the throw.
· Each row will not have the same stitch count as the other rows, because the number of stitches on a row will change, depending on where you are in the pattern repeat of each of the four stitch patterns being worked.

Cabled-feather pattern (A)
Worked over 38 sts.
Row 1 (WS) P across.
Row 2 K1, (k2tog) 3 times, (yo, k1) 6 times, (k2tog) 6 times, (yo, k1) 6 times, (k2tog) 3 times, k1.
Row 3 P1, k15, p6, k15, p1.
Row 4 K16, sl the next 3 sts to the dpn and hold at the back of the work, k3, then k3 from the dpn, k16.
Row 5 Rep row 1.
Row 6 Rep row 2.
Row 7 Rep row 3.
Row 8 K across.
Rep rows 1–8.

Clustered-braid pattern (B)

Abbreviation:

BKC – sl 2 sts to the dpn and hold at the back of the work, k2, then k2 from the dpn.

Worked over 20 sts.

Rows 1 and 3 (WS) K4, (p4, k4) twice.

Row 2 P4, BKC, p4, C2F, k2, then k2 from the dpn, p4.

Row 4 P3, 3-st BC, 3-st FC, p2, 3-st BC, 3-st FC, p3.

Row 5 and all subsequent WS rows Knit all knit sts and purl all purl sts.

Row 6 P2, (3-st BC, p2, 3-st FC) twice, p2.

Row 8 P2, k2, p4, BKC, p4, k2, p2.

Row 10 P2, k2, p4, k4, p4, k2, p2.

Row 12 Rep row 8.

Row 14 P2, (3-st FC, p2, 3-st BC) twice, p2.

Row 16 P3, 3-st FC, 3-st BC, p2, 3-st FC, 3-st BC, p3.

Row 18 Rep row 2.

Row 20 Rep row 4.

Row 22 P3, (k2, p2) twice, slip the last 6 sts worked on to the dpn and wrap the yarn 4 times counterclockwise around these 6 sts, then slip the 6 sts back on to the RH needle, p2, k2, p3.

Row 24 Rep row 16.

Rep rows 1–24.

Fancy-shell pattern (C)

Worked over 13 sts.

Row 1 (WS) K2, p1, (k1, p1) 4 times, k2.

Row 2 P2, k1, p1, ssk, k1, k2tog, p1, k1, p2.

Row 3 K2, p1, k1, p3tog, k1, p1, k2.

Row 4 P2, k1, (yo, k1) 4 times, p2.

Rep rows 1–4.

Twin-leaf pattern (D)

Abbreviation:

ssk and pass – ssk, then slip the resulting st purlwise to the LH needle and, with the point of the RH needle, pass the adjacent stitch on the LH needle over the slip stitch and off the LH needle. Then, slip the stitch back to the RH needle (a two-stitch decrease).

Worked over 22 sts.

Row 1 (WS) and all other WS rows P10, k2, p10.

Row 2 K6, ssk and pass, yo, k1, yo, p2, yo, k1, yo, sl1–k2tog–psso, k6.

Row 4 K4, ssk and pass, k1, (yo, k1) twice, p2, k1, (yo, k1) twice, sl1–k2tog–psso, k4.

Row 6 K2, ssk and pass, k2, yo, k1, yo, k2, p2, k2, yo, k1, yo, k2, sl1–k2tog–psso, k2.

Row 8 Ssk and pass, k3, yo, k1, yo, k3, p2, k3, yo, k1, yo, k3, sl1–k2tog–psso.

Rep rows 1–8.

Aran-patchwork blanket and braid throw.

Design your own

There are quite literally hundreds of stitch variations that can be used to make up your own panelled throw. Light, openwork, lacy panels can be mixed with chunky cables, intricate cables and twisted-stitch panels. The stitch patterns will always determine how many stitches are required for the width of the throw, and how many rows are needed for a repeat, so use these stitch and row numbers to work out which patterns will work best. A wide one, of, say, 16 sts, may ideally be followed by a narrower one, of around 9 sts.

There are no rules; use whichever stitch patterns appeal most to you, and your personality and creativity will shine through. All the stitches are based on four basic techniques: knitting, purling, yarning over and using a cable needle.

Sticky notes or a pencil and paper are vital when designing a throw with several panels: it is easy to lose your way if distracted. Also use the sticky notes to cover the written instructions or lines of the chart for the rows that are yet to be knitted.

Always knit a reasonably sized test block to allow you to see what the repeat will look like. Cables pull the finished fabric in, so you may need to add stitches to compensate for this effect. Openwork stitches will make the fabric looser. As you work your chosen pattern blocks, you will get a feel for the stitch pattern and the knitting rhythm that it produces. To achieve the effect you desire, you can customize stitch patterns by changing the number of rows between cables and yarnovers.

Only by playing with the patterns will you get to know what is possible, gain confidence and make an original item. There is a real joy in combining stitch patterns and colours, producing something truly unique.

To design a throw, start in the middle and work outwards; decide what is to be the main central panel, perhaps a large, chunky cable or a cable-stitch pattern. If you require a line between each panel, add a k1, p1, k1 sequence of stitches on each side of the panels. Build up the throw with another pattern on each side, and so on, until you have the required width.

Test out each stitch by working a swatch. This will help you to ascertain whether you need to add another edging stitch or another repeat. It will also help to sort out what is the RS and what is the WS of the pattern and on which row of the stitch pattern you will need to start knitting.

Method
Using 5mm needles and Duck Egg, cast on 174 sts.

Row 1 (WS) Work the first row of pattern C, followed by the first rows of the other patterns, according to this sequence: C, D, C, B, A, B, C, D, C.

On subsequent rows, continue working through the pattern repeats for each of the nine stitch-pattern panels, following the sequence C, D, C, B, A, B, C, D, C.

When the fabric measures approximately 210cm (82½in), cast off loosely.

Finishing
Sew in all yarn tails, trim the ends and block and lightly press the fabric, without flattening the texture of the cables.

Fun with colour

Little-waves cot blanket

Soft, pastel shades were used for this wave pattern, suitable for any baby. This very versatile pattern can be jazzed up with the use of primary colours only or by using up odd balls of leftover yarn of many different colours. It is an adaptation of the border pattern used in the Fair Isle 1 chart and is also used for the little-

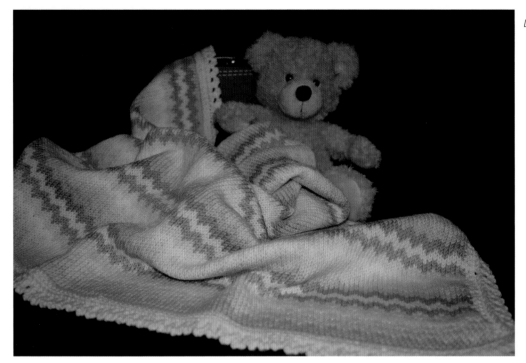

Little-waves cot blanket.

waves pots. This cot blanket is finished with edging of the openwork filigree-lace pattern, worked with a single colour of yarn.

Size
Width × length (with edging), 72cm × 86cm (28½in × 34in)

Yarn
Rowan Superfine Merino 4ply – 1 × 50g ball each of 264 Sky (A), 267 Fresh (B), 265 Minty (C), 261 Polar (D), 266 Blush (E), 269 Marble (F), 262 Cream (G) and 263 Lilac (H), for knitting the blanket, and 1 × 50g ball of 262 Cream (G), for the edging

Needles
A pair of 3.25mm (US3, UK10) straight needles

Tension
28 sts and 36 rows to 10cm (4in) over st st, after washing and pressing

Note
- Read the chart from right to left for RS rows and left to right for WS rows.
- Use the Fair Isle technique throughout, and strand the yarn across the back of the work.

A	A	A	A	A	A	A	A	A	A	A	A	24
A	A	A	H	A	A	A	H	A	A	A	H	
H	A	H	H	H	A	H	H	H	A	H	H	
H	H	H	H	H	H	H	H	H	H	H	H	
H	H	H	G	H	H	H	G	H	H	H	G	20
G	H	G	G	G	H	G	G	G	H	G	G	
G	G	G	G	G	G	G	G	G	G	G	G	
G	G	G	F	G	G	G	F	G	G	G	F	
F	G	F	F	F	G	F	F	F	G	F	F	
F	F	F	F	F	F	F	F	F	F	F	F	
F	F	F	E	F	F	F	E	F	F	F	E	
E	F	E	E	E	F	E	E	E	F	E	E	
E	E	E	E	E	E	E	E	E	E	E	E	
E	E	E	D	E	E	E	D	E	E	E	D	
D	E	D	D	D	E	D	D	D	E	D	D	10
D	D	D	D	D	D	D	D	D	D	D	D	
D	D	D	C	D	D	D	C	D	D	D	C	
C	D	C	C	C	D	C	C	C	D	C	C	
C	C	C	C	C	C	C	C	C	C	C	C	
C	C	C	B	C	C	C	B	C	C	C	B	
B	C	B	B	B	C	B	B	B	C	B	B	
B	B	B	B	B	B	B	B	B	B	B	B	
B	B	B	A	B	B	B	A	B	B	B	A	
A	B	A	A	A	B	A	A	A	B	A	A	1

Little-waves chart.

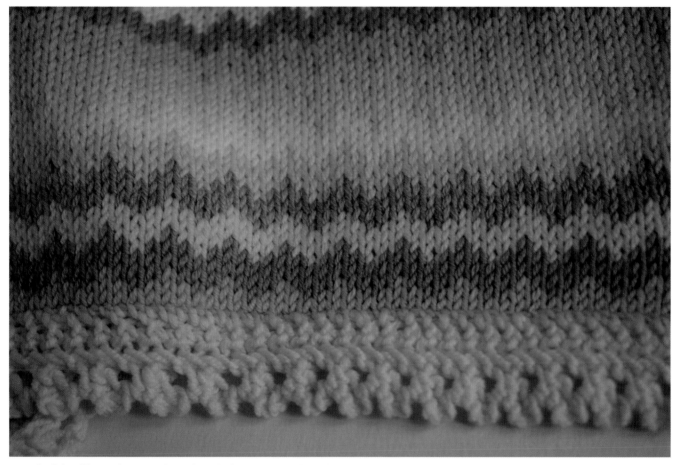
Detail of the filigree-lace edging of the little-waves cot blanket.

Method
Using 3.25mm needles and A, cast on 180 sts, and work 2 rows st st.

Work the little-waves chart, following the yarn-colour sequence A–H.

Repeat working the little-waves chart until the fabric measures 79cm (31in).

Work 2 rows st st, and cast off loosely.

Filigree-lace edging
With G, cast on 6 sts.

Row 1 K1, k2tog, yo, k2, (yo) twice, k1.

Row 2 K1, knit into the front of and then the back of the double yo of the previous row, k2tog, yo, k3.

Row 3 K1, k2tog, yo, k5.

Row 4 Cast off 2 sts, k2tog, yo, k3.

Rep rows 1–4.

Work until there is enough edging, when slightly stretched, to be sewn in place around the entire perimeter of the blanket.

Finishing
Sew in all yarn tails, trim the ends and wash, block and press the blanket.

Stitch the edging in place to the perimeter of the blanket, taking care to ease the edging around the corners, so that it will lie flat.

Neatly stitch together the cast-on and cast-off edges of the edging.

Sew in and trim all remaining yarn tails, and press the blanket again, lightly.

CHAPTER 5

POTS AND VESSELS

Decorative objects enrich our lives and, if they can be put to use, it is a bonus. The following projects are fun to make and, with practice, larger and more elaborate examples can be developed.

The first set of pots and vessels takes advantage of the fact that knitted fabric is versatile because it is so stretchy and malleable. Worked with a lightweight yarn, for example, a four-ply yarn, the fabric can be placed over a mould and stiffened with a PVA glue, to form pots and vessels.

The second set of containers, of baskets and bowls, relies on a heavier weight of yarn, for example, chunky- or aran-weight yarn, being worked tightly; the result-ant knitted fabric can then stand up on its own without requir-ing stiffening. You can always make your own thicker yarn, as I have done, by using a few lengths of a finer yarn, such as a double-knit (DK) yarn, held together when knitting.

Pots

Fair Isle pots

The following pots are six examples that all feature the Fair Isle 1 pattern. The first three were worked with Rowan Cotton Glacé, for a clear, distinct pattern, but, if a softer effect is preferred, use a hairier, wool-based yarn such as Rowan Felted Tweed.

As the pots are formed by using PVA, they are not waterproof; therefore, if the pots are to be used for housing plants, a watertight liner will be required within each pot.

OPPOSITE: Vessels and pots.

Fair Isle pots, knitted with cotton yarns.

Size
Top diameter 12cm (4¾in), depth 10cm (4in), bottom diameter 6cm (2¼in)

Yarn
Pot 1
Rowan Cotton Glacé, 100 per cent cotton – 1 × 50g ball each of 831 Dawn Grey, 868 Midnight, 849 Winsor, 850 Cobalt and 858 Aqua

Pot 2
Rowan Cotton Glacé, 100 per cent cotton – 1 × 50g ball each of 814 Shoot, 746 Nightshade, 843 Brown, 833 Ochre and 856 Mineral

Pot 3
Rowan Cotton Glacé, 100 per cent cotton – 1 × 50g ball each of 867 Precious, 828 Heather, 850 Cobalt and 831 Dawn Grey
Rowan Summerlite 4ply, 100 per cent cotton – 1 × 50g ball of 432 Aubergine

Needles
A pair of 3.25mm (US3, UK10) straight needles
A tapestry needle

Extras
PVA (approximately 200ml required per small pot)
Bowl
Cling film
Newspaper
Rubber gloves
Terracotta flower pot, or similarly sized mould, top diameter 12cm (4¾in), depth 10cm (4in), bottom diameter 6cm (2¼in)

Tension
27 sts and 30 rows = 10cm (4in) over st st, after pressing
Change needle size as necessary to gain the correct tension

Note
- The cast-on edge will become the top of the pot, and the fabric is worked towards what will become the base of the pot.
- Read the chart from right to left for RS rows and left to right for WS rows.
- When working the Fair Isle 1 chart, use the Fair Isle technique throughout, and strand the yarn across the back of the work.

Method
Using 3.25mm needles, cast on 76 sts with Dawn Grey (pot 1), Shoot (pot 2) or Aubergine (pot 3), and work 2 rows st st.

Work the Fair Isle 1 chart, following the accompanying colour key for the pot that you have decided to make.

When the chart has been completed, shape the base.

With Dawn Grey (Pot 1), Shoot (Pot 2) or Aubergine (Pot 3), work 2 rows st st.

Next row K2tog across (38 sts).

Work 3 rows st st.

Next row K2tog across (19 sts).

Work 2 rows st st.

Pot 1		Pot 2		Pot 3	
-	831 Dawn Grey	-	814 Shoot	-	432 Aubergine
/	868 Midnight	/	746 Nightshade	/	867 Precious
X	850 Cobalt	X	843 Brown	X	828 Heather
0	858 Aqua	0	833 Ochre	0	850 Cobalt
\	849 Winsor	\	856 Mineral	\	831 Dawn Grey

Colour keys for the Fair Isle 1 chart, for the Fair Isle pots.

Next row K2tog to last st, k1.

Leaving a long tail, cut the yarn, thread a tapestry needle with the yarn, pass the needle through the remaining stitches, and draw the stitches together tightly.

Finishing

Starting from the base of the pot, where the stitches have been drawn together, sew the edges of the pot together to create a firmly closed side seam.

Sew in all yarn tails, and trim the ends.

Stiffening the pots

Cover the pot mould to be used with two layers of cling film.

Pour the PVA into the bowl, and place the bowl on sheets of newspaper.

Some of the items needed for pot stiffening: PVA, a bowl and a mould covered with cling film.

BELOW: The Fair Isle pots before stiffening.

Immerse the pots in PVA.

Place the PVA-coated knitted fabric over the mould.

Wash the knitted fabric with detergent to remove any oil in the yarn and to help absorption of the PVA.

Rinse the knitted fabric well.

Turn the work inside out and immerse it into the PVA: this is a messy business. Make sure that the knitted fabric is fully coated, turn it the right way out and immerse it again in the PVA, to fully coat the outside.

Squeeze out the excess liquid from the work, and place it over the mould. At this stage, the knitted fabric is malleable and forgiving; ease it into the required shape over the mould.

Smooth out any puddling of liquid, and leave the knitted fabric on the mould, positioned over newspaper covered with cling film to catch any drips of liquid, until it is completely dry: this may take twenty-four hours. Keep checking the drying and hardening progress, wipe away any drips, and adjust the pot shape if needed.

Fair Isle pots, knitted with wool-based yarns.

When the pot is completely dry, ease it away from the form.

The featured variations of these three pots were knitted with Rowan Felted Tweed and are of the same colourways as used for the Fair Isle throw (*see* Chapter 4).

To make these pots, follow the same method as for the Fair Isle pots knitted with cotton yarns.

Little-waves pots

Any mould can be used to make these pots, providing that it does not have indents, which will cause problems when attempting to remove the dried work. To make the examples of this pattern, a beaker-shaped pot was used as the mould.

Little-waves pots.

Size
To fit a mould, top diameter 10cm (4in), depth 13cm (5in), bottom diameter 6cm (2¼in)

Yarn
Four-ply or DK yarn – small amounts of the colours that you would like to use are required

Pot 1
Rowan Felted Tweed of the colours 152 Watery, 150 Rage, 193 Cumin, 186 Tawny and 145 Treacle

Pot 2
Four-ply yarn of the colours navy, pink, lime green, yellow, white and bright blue

Pot 3
Four-ply yarn of the colours dark green, orange, lime green, pale blue, white, royal blue and yellow

Needles
A pair of 4mm (US6, UK8) straight needles
A tapestry needle

Extras
The same extras are required as for the Fair Isle pots

Tension
21 sts and 28 rows = 10cm (4in) over st st, after pressing
Change needle size as necessary to gain the correct tension

Method
Cast on 60 sts, and work 2 rows st st.

Follow the little-waves chart (see the section 'Little-waves cot blanket' in Chapter 4) to work fourteen coloured stripes or sufficient stripes to create the chosen depth for your pot.

Shape the base by following the instructions for the Fair Isle pots.

Finishing

Finish the knitted fabric and form and stiffen each pot as for the Fair Isle pots.

Landscape pot

The landscape pot was made by using various colours and shades, including aqua blue, greens, amethyst, pale blue, yellow, alabaster and delft, of Rowan Cotton Glacé, Rowan Felted Tweed and merino-wool yarns, some of which were mixed by holding two threads of yarn together and knitting them as one. This creates interesting textures and varying tensions. Experiment with garter stitch and slip stitches, and embellish with embroidery and stitching over the surface of the knitted fabric.

Collect yarns together to assess colour selections.

Landscape pot.

The technique of adding in colours of yarn as others are taken out is very creative and liberating. Know what you are trying to achieve, either from a photograph or sketch, of a landscape or seascape, and decide which colours are needed.

Collect all of the colours together of yarns that are of a similar thickness, decide which colours work well, and discard those that do not add interest or texture. Adding cream or white can allow the other colours

Try wrapping yarns around a card to help you to decide which yarns work well together.

space to breathe, while a dark blue or black can sharpen up the mid-tones and create real contrast. There is no right or wrong with this technique, as the effect will always be good. Greys, pale greens and beiges create a calm around the other colours, but if you use only this type of colour then your work may become bland.

The different way that colours interact is why it is lovely to experiment, and surprising results can be created. Try mixing a four-ply yarn with a singles lace-weight yarn, knitting them as one thread. Every knitter has a stash of spare balls of wool, so rummage around and find yarns that you have forgotten about.

Knit a tension swatch to work out how many stitches and rows you will need to make a particular size of pot.

Size
Top diameter 17cm (6¾in), depth 13.5cm (5in)

Yarn
Small amunts of 4ply, DK and aran-weight

Needles
A pair of 4mm (US6, UK8) straight needles
A tapestry needle

Extras
The same extras are required as for the Fair Isle pots

Tension
21 sts and 28 rows = 10cm (4in) over st st, after pressing

Method
Follow the instructions for the Fair Isle and little-waves pots. When you have placed the fabric on to the mould, you can also add other, thicker, aran-weight threads dipped into the PVA to build up more texture on the outside of the pot.

Finishing
When your pot is dry, apply PVA to shells and pebbles by using a paintbrush, and attach them to the sides of the pot as decoration. This can be performed while the pot is still positioned on the mould

but, if the pot has already been removed, do not saturate the fabric again with PVA: the pot is not waterproof and will start to lose its shape.

If a fine yarn has been used and the base is not very large or flat, try gluing a small coin or similar item on to the bottom to increase the pot's stability.

Bowls or baskets

Unlike the previous pots and vessels, the bowls and baskets are formed by knitting with yarn alone, because they stand up on their own. Their difference in size will depend on the thicknesses and textures of the yarns and the needle sizes that are used. Three very different bowls can be made from one basic pattern.

Peony-coloured bowl (small), embellished, green bowl (medium) and rustic, grey bowl (large).

Design your own

Try using a wonderful, chunky cable-stitch pattern for a vessel, and stiffening it with PVA. The thicker the yarn, the more PVA that you will need to use.

There are many household objects that could be used as moulds, for example, mixing bowls. Try using plates to form flat dishes or a house brick to make a box-like container.

Small bowl

Size
Diameter 8cm (3¼in), depth 6cm (2¼in)

Yarn
Rowan Felted Tweed – 1 × 50g ball each of contrasting colours such as 183 Peony and 167 Maritime, using two strands held together and knitted as one thread

Needles
A pair of 4mm (US6, UK8) straight needles
A tapestry needle

Tension
22 sts and 40 rows = 10cm (4in), using two strands of yarn held together, over garter stitch, after light pressing
   Change needle size as necessary to gain the correct tension

Medium bowl

Size
Diameter 15cm (6in), depth 10cm (4in)

Yarn
Rowan Cotton Glacé – 3 × 50g balls of 814 Shoot, using

Medium bowl without woven embellishment.

four threads of the yarn held together and knitted as one thread. To enable this, wind some of the yarn into a separate ball, allowing four ends to be available at the same time.
   Similar yarn in small amounts of shades of blue, yellow and cream, with each separate yarn threaded double, for embellishment

Needles
A pair of 5.5mm (US9, UK5) straight needles
A tapestry needle

Tension
15 sts and 12 rows = 10cm (4in), using four strands of yarn together, over garter stitch, after light pressing
   Change needle size as necessary to gain the correct tension

Large bowl

Size
Diameter 15cm (6in), depth 15cm (6in)

Yarn
Rowan Felted Tweed Aran – 2 × 50g balls of 765 Scree, for knitting the bowl, and 1 × 50g ball of 777 Clay, for embellishment, using two strands held together throughout

Needles
A pair of 7mm (US10–11, UK2) straight needles
A large tapestry needle or bodkin

Tension
10 sts and 12 rows = 10cm (4in), using two strands of yarn together, over garter stitch, after light pressing
   Change needle size as necessary to gain the correct tension

Method
Base pattern
Abbreviation:

sl1–k1–psso – slip a stitch knitwise (sl1), knit the next stitch (k1) and pass the slip stitch over (psso) (a one-stitch decrease).

Using 4mm (small bowl) (5.5mm, medium bowl) (7mm, large bowl) needles, cast on 4 sts.

Work with garter stitch throughout.

Row 1 K1, inc in the next 2 sts, k1 (6 sts).

Row 2 K1, inc in the next st, k2, inc in the next st, k1 (8 sts).

Row 3 K1, inc in the next st, k to the last 2 sts, inc in the next st, k1 (10 sts).

Row 4 Rep row 3 (12 sts).

Row 5 K across.

Row 6 Rep row 3 (14 sts).

Row 7 K across.

Row 8 Rep row 3 (16 sts).

Next rows Knit 3 (3) (4) rows.

Next row Rep row 3 (18 sts).

Next rows Knit 3 (4) (6) rows.

Next row Rep row 3 (20 sts).

Next rows Knit 5 (6) (8) rows.

Next row K1, sl1–k1–psso, knit to the last 3 sts, k2tog, k1 (18 sts).

Next rows Knit 3 (4) (6) rows.

Next row K1, sl1–k1–psso, knit to the last 3 sts, k2tog, k1 (16 sts).

Next rows Knit 3 (3) (4) rows.

Next row K1, sl1–k1–psso, knit to the last 3 sts, k2tog, k1 (14 sts).

Next row K across.

Next row K1, sl1–k1–psso, knit to the last 3 sts, k2tog, k1 (12 sts).

Next row K across.

Next 3 Rows K1, sl1–k1–psso, knit to the last 3 sts, k2tog, k1 (6 sts).

Cast off, working k2tog for the second and third sts and the fourth and fifth sts of the previous row.

Side pattern
Using 4mm (small bowl) (5.5mm, medium bowl) (7mm, large bowl) needles, cast on 12 sts.

Work with garter stitch until the side is long enough to stretch around the circumference of the base.

Cast off.

Detail of woven embellishment.

Making up
Sew together the short cast-on and cast-off edges of the sides.

Securely sew the bottom side edge to the base.

Finishing
Sew in all yarn tails, and trim the ends.

To work the woven embellishment, thread a needle or bodkin with contrasting yarn, and sew a running stitch that weaves in and out of the garter-stitch ridges. Be careful to keep the running stitch loose, and do not pull the weaving yarn taut because this will distort the shape of the basket. Offset the running stitch with the previously worked row of this stitch, until the basket is covered.

Design your own

Try using a basket-weave stitch, and change the colour of the yarn being woven after every few rows. Chunky braids and cables or any highly textured stitches can be used as the framework for weaving. A word of caution, though; make sure that you use small pattern repeats, because it will be easier to match up the seam join. The finished project will look untidy if the stitch pattern does not run around the bowl smoothly, with a near-invisible join.

CHAPTER 6

LAMPSHADES

There are many shapes of and methods for making lampshades; here, just a few of these methods are presented. Frames bought from charity shops can be upcycled by stripping them down and adding a delicate star-stitch fabric or a fabric of eyelet mock-cable stitch, knitted with cotton or wool yarn to achieve different effects.

A fine cotton yarn was used to make the shell lampshade, and it was stiffened with a solution of sugar and water, while the larger Fair Isle shade was shaped and placed over a mould, with the shape being set with PVA glue. A kit for making a drum lampshade, available from all good lampshade suppliers, was used for the seascape lampshade.

Lampshade variations

Star lampshade

This lampshade features a lovely, soft, textured, lacy pattern that resembles crochet. The delicacy of the stitch is shown to full advantage when a light-coloured cotton yarn is used and when the fabric is slightly stretched.

The lampshade used was a charity-shop buy that was stripped down to the frame, and all of the residual fabric and remaining dried glue were removed. The

cotton Oyster coloured yarn was then wrapped around the white wire frame at the top, bottom and sides. The wrapped wire was then used as a base to attach the knitted fabric.

Star lampshade.

OPPOSITE: A selection of lampshades.

Size

To fit a circular, tapered lampshade frame, top diameter 10cm (4in), height 16cm (6¼in), bottom diameter 20cm (8in)

Yarn

Rowan Cotton Glacé 100 per cent cotton – 1 × 50g ball of 730 Oyster

Needles

A pair of 3.25mm (US3, UK10) straight needles
A tapestry needle

Extras

Circular, tapered lampshade frame, top diameter 10cm (4in), height 16cm (6¼in), bottom diameter 20cm (8in)

Tension

23 sts and 32 rows = 10cm (4in) over st st, after pressing

Star-stitch pattern

Row 1 (WS) K2, * yo, k3, insert the point of the LH needle from left to right into the first of the 3 k sts, and lift it over the other 2 sts and off the RH needle (as for a psso); rep from * to the last st, k1.
Row 2 Knit all yos.
Row 3 K1, * k3, take first of the 3 k sts over the other 2 sts as before, yo; rep from * to the last 2 sts, k2.
Row 4 K across.
Rep rows 1–4.

Method

Using 3.25mm needles and Oyster, cast on 111 sts.
   Work rows 1–4 of the star-stitch pattern throughout, until the fabric measures 15cm (6in).
   Knit 1 row, and cast off.

Finishing and making up

Sew together the side edges of the fabric to form a seam, which results in a tube.
   Wrap the top, bottom and supports that form the sides of the frame with the yarn. This wrapping will be

used as a base for attachment of the knitted fabric, and it ensures a neat interior for the lampshade.

Sew in all yarn tails, and trim the ends.

Pull the tube of fabric over the shade, ensuring that there is enough fabric to wrap under the bottom and over the top of the frame, and pin it in place. With a matching colour of fine cotton thread, stitch through the bottom of the fabric on the inside, wrapped under the wire frame, through to the front of the fabric. Stitch around the entire base of the frame to secure the folded-under fabric to the front fabric. Repeat this process at the top of the lampshade frame for all of the folded-over fabric.

Sew in and trim all remaining yarn tails.

Eyelet mock-cable lampshade

For a more rustic feel, wool yarn was used for the knitted fabric of this lampshade, and the fabric features a small mock-cable pattern that is lightened with eyelets.

The colour choice was intended to be neutral, to enhance the stitch-pattern texture.

Size
To fit a rectangular, slightly tapered lampshade frame, top width 18cm (7in), height 19cm (7½in), bottom width 25cm (10in)

Yarn
Rowan Pure Wool Superwash Worsted – 1 × 100g ball of 103 Almond

Needles
A pair of 4mm (US6, UK8) straight needles
A tapestry needle

Extras
Rectangular, slightly tapered lampshade frame, top

width 18cm (7in), height 19cm (7½in), bottom width 25cm (10in). For a lampshade purchased from a charity shop for upcycling, the frame must be stripped of fabric and glue before reuse.

Tension
20 sts and 25 rows = 10cm (4in) over st st, after pressing

Eyelet mock-cable stitch pattern
Note that the stitch count does not remain the same on every row.

Detail of the inside of the covered lampshade frame.

Detail of the knitted fabric attached to the lampshade frame.

Row 1 (RS) P2, * sl 1 st, k2, psso the 2 k sts, p2; rep from * to end.
Row 2 K2, * p1, yo, p1, k2; rep from * to end.
Row 3 P2, * k3, p2; rep from * to end.
Row 4 K2, * p3, k2; rep from * to end.
Rep rows 1–4.

Method
Using 4mm needles and Almond, cast on 152 sts.

Work rows 1–4 of the eyelet mock-cable stitch pattern throughout, until the fabric measures 18cm (7in).

Cast off.

Finishing and making up
Sew together the side edges of the fabric to form a seam, which results in an oblong tube.

Wrap the top, bottom and four corner supports that form the sides of the frame with the yarn.

Sew in all yarn tails, and trim the ends.

Pull the tube of fabric over the frame, ensuing that there is enough fabric to wrap under the bottom of the frame, and pin the wrapped-under fabric at 5cm (2in) intervals to the wrapped base of the frame.

Using a tapestry needle threaded with the yarn used for knitting, stitch through the bottom of the fabric, on the inside of the frame, through to the front of the fabric.

Stitch around the entire base of the frame to secure the folded-under fabric to the front fabric.

Gently pull the fabric to the top of the frame, easing it evenly to wrap it over the top of the frame, and pin the wrapped-over fabric to the top of the frame at 5cm (2in) intervals.

Stitch the fabric into place at the top of the frame in the same manner as for the bottom of the frame.

Sew in and trim all remaining yarn tails.

Shell lampshade

The shell lampshade was made to fit on a pendant

lamp without a frame. It is made to hold its shape by stiffening the fabric with a solution of sugar and water. A delicate shell pattern is used that resembles a crocheted fabric. Fine cotton yarn and fine needles together produce a dainty lampshade.

Shell lampshade.

Size
Top diameter 11cm (4¼in), height 15cm (6in), bottom diameter 17cm (6¾in)

Yarn
Rowan Summerlite 4ply, 100 per cent cotton – 1 × 50g ball of 417 Pure White

Needles
A pair of 3mm (US2–3, UK11) straight needles
A tapestry needle

Extras
Sugar
Water
Saucepan
Mould (a plant pot turned upside down served as the mould for the example)
Cling film
Blocking board (see the section 'Blocking board' later in this pattern) or newspaper
Pins

Tension
28 sts and 36 rows= 10cm (4in) over st st, after pressing
Change needle size as necessary to gain the correct tension

Note
- If a larger, smaller or differently shaped mould is being used, you need to measure around the base of the mould and work out from your tension swatch knitted with the shell-stitch pattern how many stitches to cast on.

- Remember to take a few stitches or rows off the calculated number for the total width or length, respectively, because the fabric looks at its best when slightly stretched.
- The cast-on edge will be at the bottom of the lampshade fabric and the cast-off edge at the top.

Shell-stitch pattern
Abbreviation:
sl2–k3tog–p2sso – slip two stitches knitwise (sl2), knit the next three stitches together as one stitch (k3tog) and pass the two slip stitches over the stitch that has just been knitted (p2sso) (a four-stitch decrease).
Row 1 (WS) K1, * yo, k1; rep from * to the last st, k1.
Row 2 K across, dropping all of the yos of the previous row off the LH needle without knitting them.
Row 3 K1, k3tog, * (yo) twice, k1, (yo) twice, sl2–k3tog–p2sso; rep from * to the last 5 sts, (yo) twice, k1, (yo) twice, k3tog, k1.

Row 4 K1, * k1, knit into the front of and then the back of the double yo of the previous row; rep from * to the last 2 sts, k2.
Row 5 Rep row 1.
Row 6 Rep row 2.
Row 7 K1, * k1, (yo) twice, sl2–k3tog–p2sso, (yo) twice; rep from * to the last 2 sts, k2.
Row 8 Rep row 4.
Rep rows 1–8.

Shell lampshade saturated with sugared water, placed over the mould and pinned to a blocking board to dry.

Method

Using 3mm needles and Pure White, cast on 93 sts.

Work rows 1–8 of the shell-stitch pattern throughout, until the work measures 14cm (5½in) (or the desired depth of the lampshade).

Shaping

Next row K2tog to the last st, k1.
Next row K across.
Next row K2tog to the last st, k1.
Next row K across.
Leaving a long tail, cut the yarn, thread a tapestry needle with the yarn tail, then pass the needle through the remaining stitches to gather them, but do not draw them together too tightly; the diameter of the circle, into which the bulb housing will fit, at the top of the lampshade, should be about 3cm (1¼in).

Finishing and making up

With the long yarn tail, sew the edges of the lampshade fabric together to create a neat side seam.

Sew in all yarn tails, and trim the ends.

Stiffening the lampshade

Cover the mould with a double layer of cling film.

In a saucepan, mix equal parts of sugar and water, heat the mixture gently until the sugar dissolves, then remove the saucepan from the heat immediately, before the sugar would burn and change in colour and consistency to caramel.

Immerse the knitted fabric in the sugared water, ensuring that the fabric becomes fully saturated.

Drape and shape the fabric over the mould, pulling it gently into the required shape.

Leave the knitted fabric on the mould, positioned over newspaper covered with cling film to catch any drips of liquid, until it is completely dry. Alternatively, if you need to shape the bottom of your lampshade by pinning out the edge, use a blocking board (see the following section 'Blocking board' for details).

Do not be tempted to remove the fabric from the mould too early: it will take at least twenty-four hours to dry thoroughly.

The fabric will stiffen as it dries; however, if it gets wet again, it will lose its shape.

When the lampshade is completely dry, ease it away from the form.

Blocking board

To allow you to pin out the edge of the lampshade fabric, make your own blocking board by covering a stack of several layers of corrugated cardboard with cling film and, lastly, a tea towel. This will give you a firm base to push the pins into.

Fair Isle lampshade

This lampshade was made for a pendant light fitting. Two moulds were used, one on top of the other: an

Fair Isle lampshade.

upside-down garden pot and a little ramekin dish. They were covered with cling film. The lampshade fabric was knitted with cotton yarns of soft blues and greys, to which was added a zing of lime-green.

Size
Top diameter 8cm (3¼in), height 23cm (9in), bottom diameter 23cm (9in)

Yarn
Rowan Cotton Glacé, 100 per cent cotton – 1 × 50g ball each of 814 Shoot, 831 Grey Dawn, 850 Cobalt Blue, 858 Aqua and 746 Nightshade

Needles
A pair of 3.25mm (US3, UK10) straight needles
A tapestry needle

Extras
PVA
Bowl
Cling film
Newspaper
Rubber gloves
One or more moulds to achieve the intended lampshade shape and dimensions

Tension
23 sts and 32 rows = 10cm (4in) over st st, after pressing

Note
· The cast-on edge will be at the bottom of the lampshade fabric and the cast-off edge at the top.

Method
Using 3.25mm needles and Nightshade, cast on 120 sts, and work 6 rows st st.

Following the Fair Isle 1 chart (*see* the section 'Fair Isle cushions' in Chapter 3), complete the chart with Fair Isle colourway A, following the accompanying colour key.

Fair Isle colourway A		Fair Isle colourway B	
-	Nightshade	-	Shoot
/	Grey Dawn	/	Grey Dawn
X	Cobalt Blue	X	Cobalt Blue
0	Aqua	0	Aqua
\	Shoot	\	Nightshade

Colour keys for the Fair Isle lampshade.

Work 2 rows st st with Nightshade, decreasing by 14 sts by working a k2tog 14 times, spaced evenly across the last row only (106 sts).

Work 3 rows st st with Shoot.

Following the Fair Isle 1 chart, complete the chart with Fair Isle colourway B, following the accompanying colour key.

Work 1 row of k2tog across with Shoot (53 sts).

Work 2 rows st st with Nightshade.

Work 1 row of k2tog to the last st, k1 (27 sts).

Leaving a long tail, cut the yarn, thread a tapestry needle with the yarn tail, then pass the needle through

Fair Isle lampshade, with the mould that was used.

the remaining stitches to gather them, but do not draw them together too tightly; the diameter of the circle, into which the bulb housing will fit, at the top of the lampshade, should be about 3cm (1¼in).

Finishing and making up

With the long yarn tail, sew the edges of the lampshade fabric together to create a neat side seam.

Sew in all yarn tails, and trim the ends.

Stiffening the lampshade

Cover the mould or moulds to be used with two layers of cling film. If you are using two moulds, with one on top of the other, make sure that they are securely stacked and fully covered with the cling film.

Pour the PVA into the bowl, and place the bowl on sheets of newspaper.

Wash the knitted fabric with detergent to remove any oil in the yarn and to help absorption of the PVA.

Rinse the knitted fabric well.

Turn the work inside out and immerse it into the PVA: this is a messy business. Make sure that the knitted fabric is fully coated, turn it right way out and immerse it again in the PVA to coat the exterior fully.

Squeeze out excess liquid from the work, and place the fabric over the mould. At this stage, the knitted fabric is malleable and forgiving; ease it into the required shape over the mould, and gently pull it into shape.

Pin out the bottom edge of the lampshade fabric, first placing the mould over a blocking board, if required.

Smooth out any puddling of liquid, and leave the knitted fabric on the mould, positioned over newspaper covered with cling film to catch any drips of liquid, until it is completely dry: this may take twenty-

Fair Isle lampshade pinned out on a blocking board to dry.

four hours. Keep checking the drying and hardening progress, wipe away any drips, and adjust lampshade shape if needed.

When the lampshade is completely dry, carefully remove it by easing it away from the form; the cling film will help with the removal process.

If the lampshade is not hard all over, place the work back on to the mould, and paint some more PVA on to any unhardened spots. Leave the lampshade to dry completely.

Seascape lampshade

This lampshade was made with a bought lampshade-making kit. These kits are available for a variety of lampshade sizes and shapes, including drum, coolie and square, and are available from all good lamp-shade-making suppliers. Browse the internet to find one with the type of lampshade that you want to use in your design, decide what size and shape is required and buy the kit.

From the lampshade frame, you will be able to work out what size your knitted fabric will need to be. Work with fine, smooth, non-hairy yarn, rather than thicker, chunky yarn, as the finished fabric needs to be stuck on to a plastic sheet and tucked around and under the wire rings at the top and bottom of the lampshade.

Seascape lampshade.

The kit comes with a self-adhesive PVC panel, one metal ring each for the top and the bottom of the lampshade, a roll of double-sided tape and a finishing tool.

The fabric is worked with two thin yarns (four-ply or finer) being held together, with alternate yarns being removed and added while the piece is being knitted, so building up a seascape effect, almost by painting with the yarn. The result is a soft stripe, and the colours used were cream, pale blue, turquoise, lilac, pale green, dark blue, purple and a greeny blue: the colours of the sea on a quiet, calm day.

Size
To fit a drum-shaped lampshade frame, diameter (top and bottom) 30.5cm (12in), depth 21cm (8¼in)

The knitted fabric therefore needed to be 25cm (10in) in depth and 100cm (39in) in length after blocking and pressing

Yarn
Small amounts of 2 and 4ply yarn – approximately 150g

Needles
A pair of 2.25mm (US1, UK13) straight needles

Extras
Lampshade-making kit

Tension
26 sts and 40 rows = 10cm (4in) over st st, after pressing

Method
Cast on, and work a rectangular piece of fabric of a suitable size to cover the PVA panel of the lampshade kit. Work with two thin yarns held together at a time, removing alternate yarns and adding a different colour after every 10 rows.

Cast off.

Finishing and making up

Sew in all yarn tails, and trim the ends.

Block and press the fabric well.

Place the fabric with the right side facing down, and position the self-adhesive PVC panel over the top (on to the back of the fabric). When you are happy with the placement, peel back the release paper from the panel a little at a time, and gently press the panel on to the knitted fabric. If you detect a crease in the fabric, peel back the panel, adjust the fabric and press down the panel again. When you have completed attaching the whole length of the panel to the fabric, check once more for creases.

Snap back the PVC edges at the perforated lines parallel to the long sides of the panel, breaking off and removing the PVC edges.

Stick some double-sided tape to one of the short sides of the PVA panel. This tape will be used to stick this side to the other short side to create a seam. Remove the release paper from this tape, and set the panel to one side.

Apply double-sided tape, centred, to the top circumference of one of the metal rings. Avoid creasing the tape, press down firmly and evenly on to the metal, and pull away the release paper. Repeat this process with the other ring.

You will need to know at this stage whether you are going to use the lampshade for a table lamp or for a pendant/ceiling fitting. The utility ring (the metal ring with the circle in the middle that will contact the bulb housing) must be placed at the top of the fabric-attached panel for a pendant fitting and at the bottom for a table lamp.

Place one sticky ring on to the end (furthest away from the short side with the attached sticky tape, the seam end) of one long side edge of the PVC panel and

The sea always inspires.

the other ring on to the same end of the opposite long side, in the appropriate arrangement for the type of lampshade being made.

Start to roll both rings, at the same time, away from you and towards the seam end. This is a fiddly process and may need an extra pair of hands. Do this slowly, and keep checking whether each ring remains in line with the edge that it is being rolled along. Halfway along the long sides, turn the entire lampshade assembly by 180 degrees, and continue to roll the rings towards the seam end (towards you).

Overlap the short sides of the lampshade to form the seam, and press gently from the centre of the seam outwards to secure it. The seam will now be closed.

Turn the shade over so that the seam is on a hard surface, and press down firmly.

Pinch and gently pull the fabric along the long sides of the PVC panel over the sticky rings.

Use the finishing tool to push the fabric up and behind each ring and into the gap where the ring and panel meet. Keep pushing the fabric in this manner all around the circumference of the top and bottom rings of the lampshade frame until all of the excess fabric has been tucked in.

Design your own

Instructions have been provided for all of the lampshades in this chapter; however, these instructions are meant to be a guide only; the lampshades that you require or wish to make may be of a different size or shape. Always make the knitted fabric smaller than the frame or surface that it is to cover, because the fabric needs to be lightly stretched to look its best.

After you knit a tension swatch, experiment by pulling the fabric to see what looks best. The tension of your fabric swatch and the size measurements of your lampshade frame or of a mould that you intend to use will indicate how many stitches and rows are required and also whether any shaping is needed. The knitted fabric is very forgiving, and little shaping, if any, was used in the lampshades shown, as it was not necessary.

CHAPTER 7

RUGS, RUNNERS AND MATS

Floor furnishings

Wonderfully practical, the rugs and runners in this collection are very different in function and style. The intricate basket-weave floor mat, which could be used as a fireside rug, is worked in restrained, quiet shades of cream and beige. The clouds rug has a tough, rough, felted fabric, in soft shades of blue and grey, with stark, charcoal squares to sharpen everything up.

The seashore runner is very soft to the touch and can be used on a seat, bench or floor, or even by the bed, but it is not as hard-wearing as the previous two examples.

The Indian-print picnic runner is a complex pattern, well worth the effort and time required to make it. I go into detail regarding the choice of colour and then use the worked knitting as a basis for embroidered Swiss darning to make an even richer, embossed fabric, which is used for a chair-seat cover.

The final runner is made for the table and has matching place mats and napkin rings. Using bright, clear colours, I had in mind al-fresco dining by the sea or summer teatime in the garden.

Basket-weave floor mat

The soft basket-weave floor mat is knitted with Knoll Yarns Soft Donegal yarn.

The woven pattern twists all of the stitches on the right side of the fabric and also on the wrong side,

Detail of the basket-weave floor mat.

Basket-weave floor mat.

OPPOSITE: Clouds rug.

producing a firm, thick, textured basket weave, ideal for a floor mat.

The cream but lightly flecked yarn makes the mat versatile and possible to fit into any room. It is edged with an almond-coloured double-crochet stitch, to complete the understated look.

Size
Length × width, 104cm × 65cm (41in × 25½in)

Yarn
Knoll Yarns Soft Donegal, 100 per cent pure-merino wool – 10 × 50g balls of 5307 Swilly
Rowan Pure Wool Superwash Worsted – 1 × 100g ball of 103 Almond, for the edging

Needles
A pair of 7.5mm (US11, UK1) straight needles
A 3.5mm (US4, UK9) crochet hook

Tension
14 rows and 20 sts = 10cm (4in) over st st, after pressing

Basket-weave stitch pattern
Row 1 (WS) P2, * skip the next st on the LH needle, purl the second st on the LH needle, then purl the skipped st, slip both sts off the LH needle; rep from * to the last st, p1.
Row 2 (RS) K2, * insert the RH needle from back to front between the first and second sts on the LH needle, knit the second st, then knit the first st, then slip both sts off the LH needle; rep from * to the last st, k1.
Rep rows 1–2.

Method
Using 7.5mm needles, cast on 212 sts with the thumb method.

Work rows 1–2 of the basket-weave stitch pattern throughout, until the fabric measures 104cm (41in).

Cast off in pattern.

Detail of basket-weave stitch.

Finishing
Sew in all yarn tails, and trim the ends.

Using a 3.5mm crochet hook and Almond, work 3 rows of double crochet along one short edge of the mat (see Appendix 1 for instructions to work this embellishment), by picking up the loops of yarn to form the crochet stitches through every other gap between the knitted stitches. At the end of each row, work a turning chain by passing the yarn over the hook and pulling the yarn through the stitch on the hook, then turn the work and crochet across the next row.

Repeat working this crocheted edging for the other short edge of the mat.

Sew in and trim all remaining yarn tails.

Wash, block and press the mat.

Clouds rug

This is a striking rug made from a Donegal-tweed yarn that will be hard-wearing after it has been felted. The fleck that is a characteristic Donegal yarn makes it a favourite yarn of mine to use.

Looking at clouds on a wintry day suggested the colours that are used for this project.

Size
Length × width (after felting), 145cm × 98cm (57in × 38½in)

Yarn
Knoll Yarns Kilcarra Tweed, genuine Donegal, 100 per cent pure new wool (but any aran-weight wool yarn can be used) – 7 × 50g balls of 1443 Cream (cream, A), 3 × 50g balls each of 4596 Ballybofey (off white, C) and 4742 Ballyliffen (brown, D) and 2 × 50g balls each of 4726 Skylight (pale blue, B), 2017 Ardara (grey, E) and 4581 Milford (charcoal, F)

A note of caution, however, if you will be substituting this yarn: it must be a wool yarn, otherwise it will not felt properly

Needles
A pair of 6mm (US10, UK4) straight needles

Tension
14 sts and 16 rows = 10cm (4in) over st st, after felting

Note
- This rug is knitted with the strip method, and the strips are then sewn together.
- Strips are much easier to handle and can be easily transported, so this is an ideal project to work when you are on the go.
- Each square or oblong block is worked by knitting 34 rows of stocking stitch.
- You will notice that strips 1, 3 and 5 are all 40 sts in width, and strips 2 and 4 are narrower, being 20 sts in width.
- Strips 1 and 5 have the same colour sequence, as do strips 2 and 4.
- Try out a test swatch before you start knitting the rug; this will help you to decide how many stitches to cast on and how many rows to work to achieve the rug size that you want to knit.
- Remember that how well a knitted fabric felts will depend on the heat of the water, washing time, degree of agitation and, if using a washing machine, spin speed. The felting can be done by hand washing, but my preferred method is to use a washing machine.
- After lots of experimenting with my machine, and

everyone's is different, I use a 40°C wash, for one hour, with an 800rpm spin speed.
- For a much lighter felt, I use a 30°C wash, for 40 minutes, with an 800rpm spin speed.
- For some additional guidance, see the notes about felting with a washing machine in the section 'Felting' in Chapter 2.

Method

Using 6mm needles and following the information provided in the accompanying colour-change-sequence chart, cast on 20 sts or 40 sts, as specified, with the appropriate yarn colour for the strip being worked.

Work each block with stocking stitch over 34 rows, following the accompanying colour-change-sequence chart to complete each strip.

Cast off loosely at the end of each strip.

Making up

Sew the strips together in the correct order, using mattress stitch.

Sew in all yarn tails, and trim the ends.

Finishing

Felt the rug in a washing machine.

Remember that it is vital that you complete and felt a test swatch before putting your finished article in the washing machine.

Detail of the felted fabric of the clouds rug.

		Strip No			
Block No (each of 34 rows)		1	2	3	4	5
	12	D	F	B	F	D
	11	C	E	A	E	C
	10	B	F	D	F	B
	9	A	E	C	E	A
	8	D	F	B	F	D
	7	C	E	A	E	C
	6	B	F	D	F	B
	5	A	E	C	E	A
	4	D	F	B	F	D
	3	C	E	A	E	C
	2	B	F	D	F	B
	1	A	E	C	E	A
		40 sts	20 sts	40 sts	20 sts	40 sts

Colour-change-sequence chart for the clouds rug.

After washing and felting, pull the rug into shape; be firm at this stage, to straighten out any slant that may have developed in the fabric.

Block and steam-press the rug heavily after it has dried.

Seashore runner and cushions

The runner and cushions are knitted using a thick yarn and with the dense fabric stitch. Large needles are used so that the work does not become tight and

Seashore runner and cushions.

difficult to knit. The fabric has a lovely dense texture on both sides like that of weaving, which is ideal for furnishing fabrics.

The colours chosen reflect the seashore and a sandy beach, with a blue sky on an autumn day.

Seashore runner

Size
Width × length, 50cm × 160cm (19½in × 63in)

Yarn
Rowan Big Wool – 3 × 100g balls of 026 Blue Velvet (A) and 2 × 100g balls each of 052 Steel Blue (B), 056 Glum (C) and 082 Biscotti (D)

Needles
A pair of 7.5mm (US11, UK1) straight needles

Tension
12 sts and 23 rows = 10cm (4in) over fabric stitch, after light pressing

Fabric-stitch pattern
Row 1 (RS) K1, * sl 2 sts wyif, k2; rep from * to the last 3 sts, sl 2 sts wyif, k1.

Row 2 K1, p2, * sl 2 sts wyib, p2; rep from * to the last st, k1.

Rep rows 1–2.

Method
Using 7.5mm needles and A, cast on 60 sts.

Work 20 rows with each colour in the following sequence: A, B, C, D.

Repeat the A–D colour sequence 3 times, and work a further 20 rows with A.

Cast off.

Finishing
Sew in all yarn tails, and trim the ends.

Wash, block and press the runner.

Seashore cushions

Have fun with these cushion covers and make up your own colour combinations, to suit your own interior.

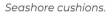*Seashore cushions.*

Size

To fit a cushion pad, 30.5cm × 30.5cm (12in × 12in) square

Yarn

Rowan Big Wool – 1 × 100g ball of 026 Blue Velvet (A) and 2 × 100g balls each of 052 Steel Blue (B), 056 Glum (C) and 082 Biscotti (D), for knitting both cushions

Needles

A pair of 7.5mm (US11, UK1) straight needles

Extras

2 × cushion pads, 30.5cm (12in) square
Optional zip (per cushion), 30.5cm (12in)

Tension

12 sts and 23 rows = 10cm (4in) over fabric stitch, after light pressing

Note

· The cushion covers are knitted throughout with fabric stitch (see the previous section, 'Seashore runner').
· The front and back of each cushion cover are knitted as one piece.

Method

Striped seashore cushion

Using 7.5mm needles and A, cast on 24 sts, work a 4-row stripe with fabric stitch, and continue working 4-row stripes with B, C and D in turn.

Repeat the A–D colour sequence until 32 rows have been completed (eight 4-row stripes), completing the front of the cushion cover.

To work the back of the cushion cover, continue working fabric stitch with D for 32 rows.

Seashore-variation cushion

The variation cushion cover is knitted with B on the front and C on the reverse.

Using B, cast on 24 sts, and work 32 rows with fabric stitch.

Using C, work a further 32 rows with fabric stitch, and cast off.

Finishing and making up (both cushions)
Sew in all yarn tails, and trim the ends.

Fold each cushion cover in half to form a square shape.

With a length of one of the yarn colours, sew together the LH edges and the RH edges to form side seams, then sew in and trim the seaming-yarn ends.

Insert the cushion pad, and either sew the entire bottom opening closed with a length of yarn or, if desired, sew in a zip with sewing thread.

Indian print

Indian-print picnic runners

No pattern is a one-trick pony; there are dozens of ways in which it can be interpreted. Think of the water-lily paintings by Monet, many painted from the same viewpoint, yet all utterly different interpretations, depending on the time of year or day, the weather and even the mood he was in. Each painting expanding Monet's knowledge of this beautiful subject.

The patterns used for these runners have been favourites for the past forty years, and they still inspire new colour interpretations.

Read completely through the pattern and all of the information in this section before you start to plan your colours.

Plan to have an even number of colours for the background and an odd number for the X colours, or vice versa; this way, the colours will travel up the pattern and not fully repeat again for a while. Many colours have been used, but this pattern is equally successful when worked with fewer colours.

The Indian-print summer-border picnic runner had as its inspiration garden borders, jam-packed with blooms, buds and leaves.

The Indian-print autumn picnic runner was inspired by a walk around the garden in September, with blackberries, elderberries and rosehips set against damp

Indian-print picnic runner.

yellow and emerald leaves, stagnant water, dark bark, olive-green and khaki moss, mauve and ruby Cotinus coggygria and lime-green spiced rocket, with its tiny ochre flowers.

Size
Width × length, 77cm × 168cm (30½in × 66in)

Yarn
The runners used a total of 600g of four-ply wool yarn. I have not given precise yarn quantities, as I hope that you will use the pattern and customize it for yourself. The instructions are very basic, so this will give ample opportunity to work out your own colourways.

Summer-border colour inspiration for the Indian-print summer-border picnic runner.

Autumn colour inspiration.

Indian-print summer-border picnic runner.

Indian-print autumn picnic runner.

Indian-print summer-border picnic runner

The background colours used are shades of blue and green, eleven different colours in all. Shades range through dark green, lime green, emerald, sky blue, peacock, navy and royal blue. The X colours range through reds to purples to yellows. There are eight different colours in total: red, cerise, violet, pink, orange, yellow, dark red and coral.

Indian-print autumn picnic runner

The background colours range through dark chocolate, muddy brown, purple, navy, ruby, dark green and emerald. The X colours are lime green, orange, red, chestnut, beige, yellow and olive green.

Needles
A 3.75mm (US5, UK9) circular needle

Tension
28 sts and 32 rows = 10cm (4in) over st st, after washing and pressing

Note
- Read the charts from right to left for RS rows and from left to right for WS rows.
- Use the Fair Isle technique throughout, and strand the yarn across the back of the work.
- A circular needle was chosen for this project because you will be working with lots of stitches. Work knit and purl rows as you would with a pair of straight needles.
- Twist yarns on WS rows to avoid a hole.

Method
Using a 3.75mm circular needle, cast on 190 sts.

For the border, * work 8 rows with garter stitch, using the edging colour that you have chosen.

Work 4 rows st st with plain colour, then work the dart-border chart.

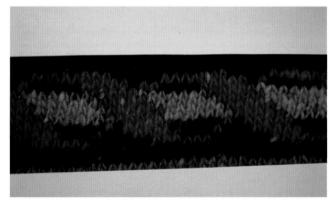

Rope border.

Indian-print chart.

Rope-border chart.

Dart border.

											X													
X	X									X	X	X													X
X	X	X							X	X	X	X	X											X	X
	X	X	X					X	X	X			X	X	X							X	X	X	
		X	X	X			X	X	X					X	X	X					X	X	X		
X			X	X	X	X	X	X				X				X	X	X	X	X	X	X			

(dart-border chart — 25 columns)

Dart-border chart.

Work 4 rows st st with plain colour, then work the rope-border chart.

Work 4 rows st st with plain colour.

Next rows ** Following the colour sequence as outlined, work the Indian-print chart, completing it 14 times in total throughout the length of the runner.

Change one colour every 4 rows, alternating changing the background colour and the X colour. So, work 8 rows with the background colour but, after 4 rows of working with a particular X colour, change to the next chosen X colour, and work 4 rows with it. This time, change the background colour, work 4 rows with it, then change the X colour. Repeat this colour-change sequence throughout the working of the Indian-print chart.

For the border, rep from ** – *, remembering to reverse the instructions, and turn the rope- and dart-border charts upside down to work from them, so that the knitted patterns will be the correct way up (a reflection of the patterns on the opposite end of the runner).

Cast off loosely.

Edging

Worked with the chosen edging colour.

Using a circular needle, with the right side of the fabric facing you, pick up 3 sts out of every 4 rows along one long edge of the runner, inserting the needle between the first and second stitch columns (counting inwards from the edge of the fabric).

Work 10 rows with garter stitch, and cast off.

Repeat working the edging for the other long edge of the runner.

Finishing

Sew in all yarn tails, and trim the ends.
Wash, block and press the runner.

Indian-print chair-seat cover

An old chair was purchased from a charity shop with a view to painting it and completing it by knitting a new seat cover. However, when looked at carefully, once the wood was cleaned and the warm, rich tones of the grain started to come to life, it was decided that it would be sacrilege to cover up the wood with paint. It also lent itself to the pattern and colours chosen for the seat cover: antique shades of an Arts and Craft era.

The torn basketwork seating was carefully removed, and a piece of plywood was cut to cover the hole, over-lapping by a few centimetres, to make a seat base. By knitting a tension swatch, I was able to work out what size of fabric would be needed, when slightly stretched across the wooden seat base. A minimum amount of shaping was required, and a few extra stitches were added because the knitted fabric was to cover a thin layer of foam stuck on to the plywood and be tucked under the base.

Indian-print seat cover and throw.

Detail of the Swiss darning on the Indian-print seat cover.

The Indian-print seat cover was knitted with four-ply wool of similar colours to those used for the Indian-print summer-border picnic runner. After being knitted, the fabric was embellished with Swiss darning. The finished depth of the chair seat cover required four repeats of the Indian-print chart.

Size
Front 36cm (14in), back 28.5cm (11in), depth 36cm (14in)

Yarn
Four-ply, wool yarn – small amounts of assorted colours

Needles
A pair of 3.75mm (US5, UK9) straight needles

Extras
Chair
Foam
Scissors or knife
Tacks and staples
Screws
Screwdriver
Hammer or staple gun

Tension

28 sts and 32 rows = 10cm (4in) over st st, after pressing

Method

With one of the background colours, cast on 96 sts.

Follow the method specified for working the Indian-print section of the Indian-print picnic runners, using the same method of colour changing, but working four chart repeats across the width of the fabric.

Cast off.

Finishing and making up

Sew in all yarn tails, trim the ends and wash, block and press the fabric.

To assemble the chair seat, stick a thin layer of foam to the seat base, then place the knitted fabric over the top of the foam and lightly pull it under the edge of the seat base.

Anchor the edges of the fabric by applying tacks and staples to secure them evenly to the underside of the base.

Screw the wooden base with its knitted covering in place to the chair.

Indian-print cushion

This cushion cover was knitted with Rowan Felted Tweed yarn, following the Indian-print chart through-out.

Size

To fit a cushion pad, 46cm × 42cm (18in × 16in)

Yarn

Rowan Felted Tweed – 1 × 50g ball each of 192 Amethyst, 170 Seafarer, 191 Granite, 172, Ancient, 178 Seasalter, 173 Duck Egg, 194 Delft, 152 Watery and 167 Maritime, for the background colours, and 196 Red Barn, 150 Rage, 154 Ginger, 183 Peony, 185 Frozen and 151 Bilberry, for the X colours

Needles

A pair of 4mm (U6, UK8) straight needles

Extras

Cushion pad, 46cm × 42cm (18in × 16in)

Tension

22 sts and 30 rows = 10cm (4in) over st st, after pressing

Method

The front and back of the cushion cover are knitted as one piece, which is later folded in half and seamed.

Indian-print cushion in the making.

Finishing and making up

Sew in all yarn tails, trim the ends and wash, block and press the fabric.

To make up the cushion, fold the cushion cover in half (the fold line will be between the fourth and fifth horizontal repeats of the Indian-print chart), then sew together the LH and RH sides of the knitted piece with mattress stitch (forming a tube of fabric).

Next, sew together the opposing sides of the cast-off edge. Insert the cushion pad, then sew together the opposing sides of the cast-on edge (alternatively, a zip can be inserted).

Table runner, place mats and napkin rings

The colours of the sea and the waves breaking on the shore are the inspiration for the choice of colours and the interesting, diagonal, woven stitch used for this dining set. The woven stitch makes a thick, firm fabric, because the stitches are twisted and crossed under and over each other.

Size

Table runner, 117cm × 28cm (46in × 11in)
Place mats × 4, 27cm × 20cm (10½in × 8in)
Napkin rings × 4, diameter 5.5cm (2in), height 4cm (1½in)

Yarn

Rowan Cotton Glacé, 100 per cent cotton – 2 × 50g balls each of 858 Aqua (A), 849 Winsor (B), 850 Cobalt (C) and 868 Midnight (D) and 1 × 50g ball of 726 Bleached (E)

Needles

A single 4.5mm (US7, UK7) straight needle or circular needle, for knitting when specified in the pattern

A single 3.25mm (US3, UK10) straight needle or circular needle, for knitting when specified in the pattern

Change needle size as necessary to gain the correct tension

Tension

22 st and 30 rows = 10cm (4in) over woven stitch, after washing and pressing

Woven-stitch pattern

Row 1 Using a 4.5mm needle, p across.
Row 2 Using a 3.25mm needle, * insert the tip of the RH needle through the first st on the LH needle as if to purl, knit the second st but do not slip it off the LH needle, then knit the first st through the back of the loop, then slip both stitches off the LH needle; rep from * to end.
Row 3 Using a 4.5mm needle, p across.
Row 4 Using a 3.25mm needle, k1, * insert the tip of the RH needle through the first st on the LH needle as if to purl, knit the second st but do not slip it off the LH needle, then knit the first st through the back of the loop, as before, then slip both stitches off the LH needle; rep from * to the last stitch, k1.

Rep rows 1–4.

Table runner

Method

Using a 3.25mm needle and A, cast on 52 sts with the thumb method.

Work rows 1–4 of the woven-stitch pattern throughout, following the colour-change sequence below:

Work 12 rows with A.
Work 8 rows with C.
Work 4 rows with E.
Work 16 rows with B.
Work 8 rows with D.
Work 16 rows with A.
Work 10 rows with D.
Work 4 rows with E.
Work 18 rows with C.
Work 8 rows with B.
Work 6 rows with A.
Work 2 rows with E.
Repeat this colour sequence from the beginning

Table runner, place mats and napkin rings.

until the fabric measures 116cm (45½in).

Cast off in pattern.

Place mats

I made four different place mats all of the same size, but each one had a slightly different colour-stripe sequence, so you can be inventive as well or follow the colour sequence specified.

Method
Using a 3.25mm needle and D, cast on 52 sts with the thumb method.

Work the woven-stitch pattern throughout, following the colour sequence below:

Work 10 rows with D.

Work 4 rows with E.

Work 18 rows with C.

Work 8 rows with B.

Work 6 rows with A.

Work 2 rows with E.

Work 10 rows with C.

Work 22 rows with B.

Work 4 rows with A.

Work as established until the fabric measures 20cm (8in).

Cast off in pattern. Make another three place mats, to create a set of four mats.

Napkin rings

Method
Work one napkin ring each with A, B, C and D, respectively.

Using a 3.25mm needle, cast on 26 sts.

Work 10 rows of the woven-stitch pattern.

Cast off in pattern.

Making up (napkin rings only)
Sew together the short LH and RH sides of the fabric, to form a circle.

Finishing (all items)
Sew in all yarn tails, trim the ends, and block and steam-press the fabric (avoid forming fold creases on the napkin rings).

Design your own

Change the stitch pattern: use a Fair Isle pattern, or add stripes of different Fair Isle patterns, use a single colour, work a mock-cable stitch pattern or select another pattern. Make sure that the pattern you choose produces a close, dense fabric, to protect your table surface, because warm plates may be placed on the fabric surface.

CHAPTER 8

GIFT IDEAS

All of the projects in this chapter are fun and could lead on to many other ideas and options that can be knitted. The tea and cafetière cosies, dishcloths and facecloths, and hot-water-bottle covers make wonderful presents, and adding one of the celebration cards would result in a gift of thoughtful perfection.

The director's chair covers and deckchair cover, on a practical level, liven up tired and mundane canvas covers. The warmth and comfort of sitting on knitted fabric in the garden, surrounded by nature, is an experience second to none.

Time for tea

Tea cosies were first knitted in Victorian times, and the patterns used then are still in use today. Various combinations of stitches and shapes have been used, but the most successful fabrics are made with wool, as it has excellent insulating properties.

Patterns regularly feature in knitting magazines around Christmas time, to be made as excellent presents or for sale at school fairs. They are a perfect way to use up small balls of yarn. Many years ago, a reporter from the

OPPOSITE: Wrapped-up facecloths.

Tea cosy.

Telegraph visited the cathedral shop in Worcester, where the volunteers had a cabinet full of knitted items for sale, including knitted hats topped with pom-poms and holes for asymmetrical ears!

Tea cosy

This tea cosy features a traditional stitch, which has been updated simply by the use of jewel colours of yarn. It is a useful pattern to use up oddments of yarn. The example was made with many colours of Rowan Felted Tweed yarn. The cosy can also be made with only two yarn colours, alternating across the fabric. The pleats are formed by each yarn colour being pulled gently across the back of the knitting that has just been worked with a different colour and by keeping all of the floats on the wrong side. This stitch would also make a lovely, creative cushion cover or, if worked with a thicker, chunky yarn, a rug.

Size
To fit a medium-sized teapot with a handle attached to the back (not top)

Yarn
Rowan Felted Tweed – oddments of 152 Watery (A), 183 Peony (B), 178 Seasalter (C), 150 Rage (D), 161 Avocado (E), 170 Seafarer (F), 154 Ginger (G), 192 Amethyst (H), 193 Cumin (I), 181 Mineral (J), 158 Pine (K), 185 Frozen (L), 196 Barn Red (M), 186 Tawny (N), 167 Maritime (O), 184 Celadon (P) and 151 Bilberry (Q)

Needles
A pair of 2.75mm (US2, UK12) straight needles
A pair of 3.25mm (US3, UK10) straight needles
These needles are deliberately smaller than those usually used for this DK thickness of yarn, to gain a firm fabric

Extras
Card, scissors, tapestry needle and additional yarn for pom-pom making (*see* Appendix 1 for instructions to work this embellishment)

Tension
16 sts and 23 rows = 10cm (4in) over garter st, after light pressing

Note
· The tea cosy is worked as two identical side panels that are later seamed together.
· The cosy is worked with garter stitch throughout.

Method
Using 2.75mm needles and A, cast on 98 sts.
    Work 5 rows with garter stitch.
    Changing to 3.25mm needles and B and C, work in pattern as follows:

Row 1 K1 with C, k6 with B, * k7 with C, k7 with B; rep from * to the last 7 sts, k6 with C, k1 with B.
Row 2 K1 with B, k6 with C, * k7 with B, k7 with C; rep from * to the last 7 sts, k6 with B, k1 with C.
Row 3–6 Rep rows 1–2 twice.
Change to working with D and E.
Row 7 K1 with D, k6 with E, * k7 with D, k7 with E; rep from * to the last 7 sts, k6 with D, k1 with E.
Row 8 K1 with E, k6 with D, * k7 with E, k7 with D; rep from * to the last 7 sts, k6 with E, k1 with D.
Row 9–12 Rep rows 7–8 twice.

Change to working with F and G.
    These 12 rows and colour changes form the pattern repeat.
    Work the pattern repeat 4 more times, following the colour sequence of working with F and G, H and I, J and K, L and M, N and O, P and B, Q and A, C and D.
    Changing to working with I and G, work the following top shaping:
    Next row K2tog with I, k1 with G, k2tog with G * k2tog with I, k1 with I, k2tog with I, k2tog with G, k1 with G, k2tog with G; rep from * to the last 5 sts, k2tog with I, k1 with I, k2tog with G.

Cafetière cosy and mug cosies.

Next row K1 with G, G, *k3 with G, k3 with I; rep from * to the last 3 sts, k2 with G, k1 with I.

Next row K2tog with I, k1 with G, * k2tog with I, k1 with I, k2tog with G, k1 with G; rep from * to the last 3 sts, k2tog with I, k1 with G.

Next row K1 with G, k1 with I, * k2 with G, k2 with I; rep from * to the last 2 sts k1 with G, k1 with I.

Next row (K2tog with I) twice, * k2tog with G, k2tog with I; rep from * to the last 4 sts, (k2tog) twice with G.

Cut the yarns, thread a tapestry needle with the yarns, pass the needle through the remaining stitches and draw the stitches together tightly.

Make an identical panel.

Finishing and making up

Sew in all yarn tails, and trim the ends.

Stitch the two side seams, leaving appropriately sized holes to fit the teapot spout and handle through.

Make two pom-poms of different sizes, with any of the colours of yarn used (see Appendix 1 for instructions to work this embellishment).

Attach the pom-poms to the top of the tea cosy.

Sew in and trim all remaining yarn tails.

Cafetière cosy and mug cosies

Cafetière and mug cosies are fairly recent additions to the household; however, all of the previously given reasons as to why the tea cosy has remained in fashion apply to these cosies. They are fun to make and quick, using up oddments of yarn.

Size

To fit an eight-cup cafetière
To fit a mug, top and bottom diameter 8cm (3¼in), depth 9cm (3½in)

Yarn

Rowan Felted Tweed – 1 × 50g ball each of 193 Cumin (A), 161 Avocado (B) 181 Mineral (C) and 154 Ginger (D)

Needles

A pair of 3.75mm (US5, UK9) straight needles

Extras

Button × 4 (2 × buttons for the cafetière cosy and 1 x button per mug cosy)

Tension

21 sts and 30 rows = 10cm (4in) over st st, after washing and pressing

Coin-stitch pattern

Coin stitch is so called because the resultant fabric features lots of little, offset circles that look like coins. Worked over a multiple of 4 sts plus 1 st.

Row 1 (WS) With A, p across.

Rows 2 and 4 With B, k across.

Rows 3 and 5 With B, p across.

Row 6 With A, k2, * drop the next st off the LH needle, unravel the st 4 rows down, pick up the A-coloured st from row 1 below with the LH needle, insert the RH needle into this st and under the four loose B-coloured yarn strands and knit the st (gathering up the four loose strands behind it), k3; rep from * to the last 2 sts, k2.

Row 7 With A, p across.

Rows 8 and 10 With C, k across.

Rows 9 and 11 With C, p across.

Row 12 With A, k4, * drop the next st off the LH needle, unravel the st 4 rows down, pick up the A-coloured st from row 7 below with the LH needle, insert the RH needle into this st and under the four loose C-coloured yarn strands, knit the st, k3; rep from * to the last st, k1. Rep rows 1–12.

Cafetière cosy

Method

Using 3.75mm needles and A, cast on 61 sts.

Work rows 1–12 of the coin-stitch pattern, working the coins with B, C and D in turn.

Continue as established until the fabric measures 19cm (7½in), finishing with the completion of a coin with A.

Cast off loosely.

Finishing and making up

Sew in all yarn tails, trim the ends and wash, block and lightly press the fabric (avoid forming fold creases on the cosy).

Sew together the LH and RH sides of the fabric 3cm (1¼in) down from the top edge and up from the bottom edge to form partial side seams (leaving a slit to fit the handle through).

With A, sew two buttons to one side of the handle slit, so that they will be positioned appropriately beneath the arch of your cafetière's handle, to allow fastening.

With A, sew loops to the opposite side of the slit, to go around the buttons.

Sew in and trim all remaining yarn tails.

Mug cosies

Method

For the first cosy, using 3.75mm needles and D, cast on 45 sts.

Use D as the main colour and A, B and C for working the coins.

Work the coin-stitch pattern until 5 coins have been completed.

Cast off.

For the second mug cosy, use B as the main colour and A, C and D for working the coins, following the method for the first cosy.

Finishing and making up

Sew in all yarn tails, trim the ends and wash, block and lightly press the fabric.

With the appropriate main-colour yarn, sew one button to one side of the handle slit on each mug cosy, so that it will be positioned appropriately beneath the arch of the mug handle, to allow fastening.

With the appropriate main-colour yarn, sew a loop to the opposite side of the slit, to go around the button.

Sew in and trim all remaining yarn tails.

Dishcloths and facecloths

This is a great project to try out some stitches and get to know slip stitches and twisted stitches, and their versatility.

A delicate but dense textured fabric is required for these little facecloths, and slip-stitch patterns are ideal for this purpose.

The twisted-stitch mock cable, so called because a cable needle is not required to make it, can be worked singly or as an all-over stitch pattern.

As the stitches pull together and draw in the fabric,

Stitch details of the dishcloths and facecloths.

much as with cables, make sure that enough stitches are cast on to compensate for this effect.

Rather than make four cloths of the same size, the mock-cable ones are of a larger size. Each cloth uses approximately one ball of Rowan Cotton Glacé, and the needle size remains the same regardless of the stitch pattern being worked.

Fold up the cloths and tie round a piece of ribbon or decorative string to present these items as a gift.

Size
Approximately 18cm (7in) square, for the smaller, all-over-texture cloths
Approximately 22cm (8½in) square, for the larger, mock-cable cloths

Yarn
Rowan Cotton Glacé, 100 per cent cotton – 1 × 50g ball of 730 Oyster, for each cloth

Needles
A pair of 3.25mm (US3, UK10) straight needles

Tension
23 sts and 32 rows = 10cm (4in) over st st, after pressing

Little-herringbone-stitch cloth

Method
Using 3.25mm needles and Oyster, cast on 67 sts.

Work the little-herringbone-stitch pattern as follows:
Row 1 (WS) * P2tog, leaving the stitches on the LH needle; purl the first st again, then drop both stitches together from the LH needle; rep from * to the last st, p1.
Row 2 * Sl 1 st wyib, k1, lift up the slip stitch with the LH needle (to make space to work the next step, but do not drop the k1 st from the LH needle), knit into the back loop of the lifted st by wrapping the yarn around the RH needle and pulling that wrapped yarn through the lifted st, drop the lifted st from the LH needle; rep from * to the last st, k1.

Rep rows 1–2 until the fabric measures 18cm (7in).
Cast off in pattern.

To work a larger or smaller cloth, cast on an odd number of stitches, to ensure that the stitch pattern can repeat correctly.

Close-stitch cloth

Method
Using 3.25mm needles and Oyster, cast on 61 sts.
Work the close-stitch pattern as follows:

Row 1 (WS) K across.
Row 2 K1, * sl 1 st wyib, k1; rep from * to end.
Rep rows 1–2 until the fabric measures 19cm (7½in).
Cast off.
To work a larger or smaller cloth, cast on an odd number of stitches, to ensure that the stitch pattern can repeat correctly.

Three-stitch-twist mock-cable cloth

Method
Using 3.25mm needles and Oyster, cast on 77 sts.
Work the three-stitch-twist mock-cable pattern as follows:

Rows 1 and 3 (WS) * K2, p3, k2; rep from * to end.
Row 2 * P2, k3, p2; rep from * to end.
Row 4 * P2, knit into the third st on the LH needle, then into the second st, then into the first st, then drop all 3 sts from the LH needle, p2; rep from * to end.
Rep rows 1–4 until the fabric measures 22cm (8½in).
Cast off in pattern.

Four-stitch-twist mock-cable cloth

Method
Using 3.25mm needles and Oyster, cast on 80 sts.
  Work the four-stitch-twist mock-cable pattern as follows:

Rows 1, 3 and 5 (WS) * K2, p4, k2; rep from * to end.
Rows 2 and 4 * P2, k4, p2; rep from * to end.
Row 6 * P2, knit into the fourth st on the LH needle, then into the third, second and first sts in turn, then drop all 4 sts from the LH needle, p2; rep from * to end.
Rep rows 1–6 until the fabric measures 22cm (8½in).
Cast off in pattern.

Finishing (all cloths)
Sew in all yarn tails, and trim the ends.
  Wash, block and press each cloth.

Hot-water-bottle covers

Cable-and-bobble hot-water-bottle cover

There is nothing like snuggling up to a soft and warm hot-water bottle on a cold night. Cables are so versatile and will produce a wonderful chunky texture for your work, and including a bobble will add further interest.

Two hot-water-bottle covers: a crunchy, bobbly, cabled fabric and a softer fabric featuring a cherub.

Design your own

There are hundreds of stitch patterns available to use for this project. It is a good option for investigating new stitches and trying out ideas. Cotton yarn is best to use for these cloths, as it will stand up to being wet, immersed in hot water and dried many times over.

By altering the number of rows between each cable, an eccentric cable will be produced.

This pattern uses the cable-needle technique, with an added knitted bobble. Bobbles are achieved by increasing into a single stitch, then, by turning the work, working across these increase stitches only and back across them. For most bobbles, the work is turned four times, then the bobble stitches are decreased back to a single stitch, before continuing to work the rest of the row. In this pattern, the bobble stitches are knitted and purled to increase their textural effect.

Cable-and-bobble hot-water-bottle cover.

Size
To fit a standard hot-water bottle, 20.5cm × 25.5cm (8in × 10in)

Yarn
Rowan Pure Wool Superwash Worsted – 2 × 100g balls of 112 Moonstone

Needles
A pair of 4.5mm (US7, UK7) straight needles
A 3.75mm (US5, UK9) dpn, for cabling

Detail of the cable-and-bobble stitch.

Tension
20 sts and 25 rows = 10cm (4in) over st st, after washing and a light pressing

Note
- The hot-water-bottle cover is worked as two side panels that are later seamed together.
- The cover is worked with the cable-and-bobble stitch pattern throughout.

Cable-and-bobble stitch pattern
Worked over 11 sts.
Row 1 (WS) and all other WS rows K2, p7, k2.
Row 2 P2, sl 3 sts to the dpn and hold at the back of the work, k4, then k3 from the dpn, p2.
Row 4 P2, k7, p2.
Rows 6, 10 and 12 Rep row 4.
Row 8 Rep row 2.
Row 14 P2, k3, make a bobble in the centre stitch as follows: (k1, yo, k1, yo, k1) in the same st (making 5 sts from one); turn and k5; turn and p5; turn and ssk, k1, k2tog; and turn and p3tog (which completes the bobble), then k3, p2.
Row 16 Rep row 4.
Rep rows 1–16.

Method
Using 4.5mm needles and Moonstone, cast on 38 sts.
   Work rows 1–2 of the cable-and-bobble stitch pattern.
   Keeping the cable-and-bobble stitch pattern correct while working the following rows, shape the base of the cover as follows: inc 1 st at the beginning of the next 18 rows (56 sts).
   Work straight, without shaping, until the fabric measures 25.5cm (10in).
   Next 6 rows Dec 1 st at the beginning of each row.
   Next 4 rows Cast off 4 sts at the beginning of each row.
   Next 2 rows Cast off 3 sts at the beginning of each row (28 sts).
   For the neck of the hot-water-bottle cover, work k2, p2 rib across each row, until the ribbing measures 19cm (7½in).

Cast off loosely in pattern.
Make an identical side panel.

Finishing and making up
Sew in all yarn tails, trim the ends and wash, block and lightly press the fabric, without distorting the ribbing.
   With a long length of yarn, sew the two side panels together, starting at the top of one side of the ribbing, going down one side, across the bottom and up the other side of the body of the hot-water-bottle cover and ending at the top of the opposite of the ribbing.
   Sew in and trim all remaining yarn tails.

Cherub hot-water-bottle cover

Cherub hot-water-bottle cover.

Cherub chart.

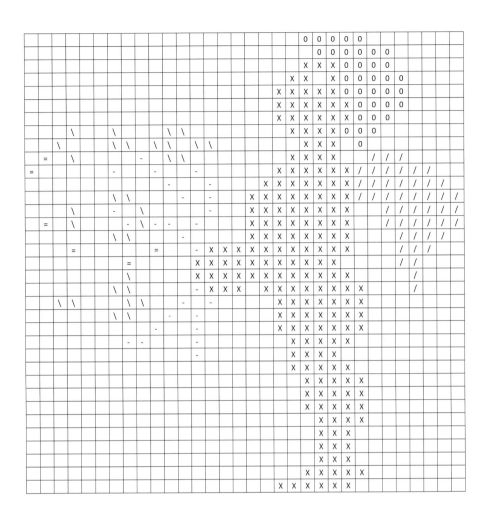

Size
To fit a standard hot-water bottle, 20.5cm × 25.5cm (8in × 10in)

Yarn
Rowan Pure Wool Superwash Worsted – 1 × 100g ball of 102 Soft Cream and a small amount each of pink, beige, yellow, red and green yarn of the same thickness

The example was worked with Rowan Felted Tweed 175 Cinnamon, 150 Rage, 184 Celadon, 181 Mineral, 185 Frozen and 152 Watery.

Needles
A pair of 4.5mm (US7, UK7) straight needles

Tension
20 sts and 25 rows = 10cm (4in) over st st, after washing and pressing

Note
· Read the charts from right to left for RS rows and left to right for WS rows.
· Use the intarsia technique, with short lengths of yarn.
· Twist the yarns around each other when changing yarn colours, to avoid a hole.
· Use sticky notes to help you to keep track of the row that you are currently working.

	X	X	X			X	X	X				13
	X	X	X	X		X	X	X	X			12
X	X	X	X	X	X	X	X	X	X	X		11
X	X	X	X	X	X	X	X	X	X	X		10
X	X	X	X	X	X	X	X	X	X	X	X	9
X	X	X	X	X	X	X	X	X	X	X	X	8
	X	X	X	X	X	X	X	X	X	X		7
	X	X	X	X	X	X	X	X	X	X		6
		X	X	X	X	X	X	X	X			5
			X	X	X	X	X	X				4
				X	X	X	X	X				3
					X	X	X					2
						X						1

Heart chart for the cherub hot-water-bottle cover.

Method

Cherub side panel

Using 4.5mm needles and Soft Cream, cast on 28 sts.

Starting with a knit row and working with st st throughout, shape the base of the cover as follows: inc 1 st at the beginning of the next 14 rows (42 sts).

Next, k5 with Soft Cream, work the first row of the cherub chart (following the accompanying colour key), then k5 with Soft Cream.

☐	Soft Cream
X	Frozen
/	Cinnamon
0	Mineral
-	Celadon
\	Rage
=	Watery

Colour key for the cherub chart.

Continue as established, following the cherub chart and working the sts on each side of the chart with st st and Soft Cream.

When the cherub chart has been completed, work 8 rows st st with Soft Cream.

Shape the panel, to form the hot-water-bottle's shoulders, as follows:

Next 4 rows Dec 1 st at the beginning of each row.

Next 4 rows Cast off 2 sts at the beginning of each row.

Next 2 rows Cast off 4 sts at the beginning of each row (22 sts).

For the neck of the hot-water-bottle cover, work k2, p2 rib across each row, until the ribbing measures 19cm (7½in).

Cast off loosely in pattern.

Heart side panel

Using 4.5mm needles and Soft Cream, cast on 28 sts.

Starting with a knit row and working with st st throughout, shape the base of the cover as follows: inc 1 st at the beginning of the next 14 rows (42 sts).

Work 26 rows st st with Soft Cream.

Next, k14 with Soft Cream, work the first row of the heart chart with Soft Cream and X = Frozen, then k15 with Soft Cream.

Continue as established, following the heart chart and working the sts on each side of the chart with st st and Soft Cream.

When the heart chart has been completed, work 4 rows st st with Soft Cream.

Shape the panel, to form the hot-water-bottle's shoulders, as follows:

Next 4 rows Dec 1 st at the beginning of each row.

Next 4 rows Cast off 2 sts at the beginning of each row.

Next 2 rows Cast off 4 sts at the beginning of each row (22 sts).

For the neck of the hot-water-bottle cover, work k2, p2 rib across each row, until the ribbing measures 19cm (7½in).

Cast off loosely in pattern.

Reverse side of the cherub hot-water-bottle cover, featuring a heart.

Finishing and making up

Embroider the cherub's eye with a colour of yarn of your choice.

Sew in all yarn tails, trim the ends and wash, block and lightly press the fabric, without distorting the ribbing.

With a long length of yarn, sew the two side panels together, starting at the top of one side of the ribbing, going down one side, across the bottom and up the other side of the body of the hot-water-bottle cover and ending at the top of the opposite of the ribbing.

Sew in and trim all remaining yarn tails.

Design your own

You can Swiss darn the flowers and stalks and add a lot more of your own details. Consider adding extra hearts, or stars, of various colours, all over the panels of the hot-water-bottle cover.

Notes and sketches of trees, together with the resulting bark chart.

Chair covers

Bark director's chair

Many photographs were taken and sketches made to allow me to design the cover for this chair. The intention was to extend the idea of painting with yarn and mix fluffy wool with firm cotton, with bright, clear

Colour inspiration for the cover of the bark director's chair.

Bark director's chair.

Yarn

Rowan Felted Tweed – 2 × 50g balls each of 145 Treacle, 193 Cumin, 157 Camel and 196 Barn Red

Rowan Cotton Glacé – 1 × 50g ball each of 814 Shoot, 739 Dijon and 730 Oyster

Rowan Summerlite DK – 1 x 50g ball each of 461 Khaki, 451 Mocha, 453 Summer and 463 Pear

Needles

A pair of 3.25mm (US8, UK10) straight needles

Extras

Director's chair
Sewing thread or Velcro® (the traditional or sticky-back version)
Scissors

colours contrasting with tweedy, soft tones. Having studied various trees and their barks, the stitch pattern is based on a combination of all of them.

To make the bark director's chair cover, swatches were knitted to ascertain which yarns and colours worked well together. The result was that Rowan Felted Tweed was chosen for the background colours and Rowan Cotton Glacé and Summerlite DK for the texture (the X stitches of the chart pattern).

Size

Every chair seems to differ in size; however, the model used for the sample is widely available from furnishing stores and garden centres. The method below outlines how to produce the pattern of the knitted fabric, but a tension swatch will have to be knitted and the appropriate size of fabric be worked out (including the number of stitches to cast on and rows to work) for the chair you are using. As knitted fabrics are stretchy, the canvas of the chair is used as a base: the knitted cover is pulled over the top of the canvas and is secured with Velcro®.

Tension

25 sts and 30 rows = 10cm (4in) over st st, after washing and pressing

Note

- Read the chart from right to left for RS rows and left to right for WS rows.
- Use the Fair Isle technique throughout, and strand the yarn across the back of the work.

Back panel

Using 3.25mm needles and Treacle, cast on, and work 2 rows st st.

Following the bark chart and using the Fair Isle technique, use the following colour sequence:

Work 10 rows with Treacle and X = Shoot.
Work 10 rows with Cumin and X =Shoot.
Work 10 rows with Cumin and X = Khaki.
Work 10 rows with Camel and X = Khaki.
Work 10 rows with Camel and X = Mocha.

Bark chart.

Work 10 rows with Barn Red and X = Mocha.
Work 10 rows with Barn Red and X = Dijon.
Work 10 rows with Treacle and X = Dijon.
Work 10 rows with Treacle and X = Oyster.
Work 10 rows with Cumin and X = Oyster.
Work 10 rows with Cumin and X = Shoot.
Work 10 rows with Camel and X = Shoot.
Work 10 rows with Camel and X =Summer.
Work 10 rows with Barn Red and X = Summer.
Cast off.

Finishing and making up

Sew in all yarn tails, trim the ends, and wash, block and press the knitted fabric.

Fold the fabric in half so that the cast-on and cast-off edges meet, and sew together the LH-side edges and then the RH-side edges, ensuring that the seamed fabric will fit over the back of your chair.

Pull the knitted panel over the canvas back panel to ascertain where the Velcro® needs to be placed, to secure the knitted cover in place.

Cut a small oblong shape of the paired Velcro® strip, and sew or stick one side of the Velcro® strip to the inside of the knitted-fabric cover, and sew or stick the other side of the strip in place on the corresponding inside face of the fabric.

Sew or stick on another pair of Velcro® strips if required.

Seat panel

For the upper side of the seat panel, cast on and work as for the back panel, but continue by adding the following rows after completing the back-panel colour sequence, for extra length:

Work 10 rows with Barn Red and X = Pear.
Work 10 rows with Treacle and X = Pear.

For the underside of the seat panel, work 10 rows st st with Treacle.

Continue by working 20-row stripes of st st using the following colour sequence: Red Barn, Cumin, Camel.

Continue with the established stripe colour sequence until the underside of the seat panel measures the same as the upper side.

Cast off.

Finishing and making up

Sew in all yarn tails, trim the ends, and wash, block and press the knitted fabric.

Fold the fabric in half so that the cast-on and cast-off edges meet.

Cut a length of paired Velcro® strip that is as long as the width of the seat cover, to join the cast-on and cast-off edges together, and sew on or stick on the strips.

With the fabric still folded in half and the seat-width Velcro® secured, turn the seat cover inside out.

Cut several 3cm (1¼in) lengths of paired Velcro® strip.

Sew or stick one side of each Velcro® strip in place along one edge of a LH-side layer of the folded knitted-fabric seat cover (the Velcro® must be placed so that it cannot be seen when the seat cover is the right way out), turn the folded seat cover over, then sew or stick the other side of each strip in place on the other layer of the LH-side fabric, so that the halves of each Velcro® strip line up, to keep the two layers of the LH side of the seat cover together.

Repeat sewing or sticking on paired Velcro® strips for the RH-side layers of fabric, so that the seat cover will be secured in place when it is turned the right way out and fitted over the canvas seat.

Landscape director's chair

Two strands of cotton are knitted as one thread throughout; for the sample, combinations of Rowan Summerlite DK and Cotton Glacé were used. This is such a free way of knitting: anything goes with putting colours

Knitted fabric for the landscape director's chair, together with the yarns that were used.

together, and it is interesting to see what works well. A splash of a bright shade like an acid lemon, here representing aconite flowers, can invigorate a dull area, while mixing brown and greens produces a calmer area.

Size
Again, each chair is different, and it is essential to knit a tension swatch to determine how many stitches to cast on and how many rows to work in order to fit the canvas fabric of your chair

Yarn
Rowan Summerlite DK – 1 × 50g ball each of 463 Pear, 461 Khaki, 457 Lagoon and 454 Mushroom

Rowan Cotton Glacé – 1 × 50g ball each of 814 Shoot, 730 Oyster, 832 Persimmon and 812 Ivy

Needles
A pair of 3.75mm (US5, UK9) straight needles

Extras
Director's chair
Sewing thread or Velcro® (the traditional or sticky-back version)
Scissors

Cover for the landscape director's chair.

Tension
16 sts and 26 rows = 10cm (4in), using two strands (one of each yarn type) together, over st st, after washing and pressing

Method
Using 3.75mm needles, cast on with two threads (one of A and one of B), for example, A = Rowan Cotton Glacé Shoot and B = Rowan Cotton Glacé Oyster.

Work 10 rows st st, then change A to another colour in your palette.

Work 10 rows st st, then change B to another colour in your palette.

Work through all of the selected yarn colours in a fairly random way, to make a lively and interesting fabric.

Finishing and making up
Finish and make up the back panel and seat panel as for the bark director's chair.

Seascape deckchair cover

Choose which colours to use, and knit a tension swatch; you can then calculate what size is needed to cover the canvas seat, with an extra 3cm (1¼in) on all sides for turning under the sides and over the top and bottom edges and being stitched with strong sewing thread to the canvas base of your deckchair.

For the sample, a strip was knitted with various shades of purple, bright blue and aqua DK and four-ply, cotton yarns, with Rowan Felted Tweed yarns of shades of blue mixed in.

Get out your stash, and put some colours together: see what works best. It may be that, when you are knitting, some of your chosen colours change, but do have an idea and a rough plan before you start working the fabric.

Size
Each chair is different, so it is essential to knit a tension swatch to determine how many stitches and rows to work in order to fit the canvas fabric of the chair

Yarn
Rowan Cotton Glacé 1 × 50g ball of 858 Aqua, 850 Cobalt, 868 Midnight, 867 Precious Rowan Summerlite DK, 457 Lagoon, 450 Indigo; Rowan Felted Tweed, 178 Seasalter, 173 Duck Egg

Seascape deckchair cover, together with the yarns that were used.

Seascape deckchair cover.

Needles
A pair of 3.75mm (US5, UK9) straight needles

Extras
Deckchair
Sewing thread or Velcro® (the traditional or sticky-back version)
Scissors

Tension
16 sts and 26 rows = 10cm (4in) over st st, after pressing

Method
Cast on using two threads (one of A and one of B), for example, A = Rowan Felted Tweed Seafarer and B = Rowan Cotton Glacé Cobalt Blue.

Work 10 rows st st, then change A to another colour in your palette.

Work 10 rows st st, then change B to another colour in your palette.

Work through all of the selected yarn colours in a fairly random way, to make an interesting and unique textured fabric.

Cast off.

Finishing and making up
Sew in all yarn tails, trim the ends, and wash, block and press the knitted fabric.

The finished fabric needs to be attached firmly to the canvas base of the deckchair. You can hand stitch the long edges of the fabric to the side edges of the deckchair canvas, and tuck the shorter top and bottom edges under and over the top and bottom of the

Design your own

Cushions and blocks for a throw can be knitted using this pattern. You can also change the yarns from thick to thin, mix cotton and wool together and work with some textured stitches. The combinations are endless; as you knit, you will be adding to your knowledge of what works well and appeals to you.

Celebration cards.

deckchair frame, then stitch them to the canvas. Alternatively, use sewn-on or sticky-back Velcro®.

Celebration cards and bunting

Sometimes little projects are excellent to have as a bit of light relief after a particularly taxing project, and the following patterns are ideal for this purpose. They also use up oddments of yarn, which can in turn produce surprising colour combinations.

Cards

Blank cards can be bought from any good stationers. It is desirable that they have an aperture; however, you can always cut your own with a scalpel blade.

If the aperture is too large for the knitted piece, add a mount of differently coloured card.

The knitted pieces for the cards shown were knitted with four-ply wool yarns.

Take the opportunity to embellish your knitting with Swiss darning. The black cat becomes a ginger tom with a colour change for the yarn, and details of crosses and flashing eyes finish off the design. The

Christmas tree is full of decorations, and a star is placed on the top, by working a combination of Swiss darning and embroidery stitches. The flower has larger Swiss-darned stitches that are sewn over two rows, using bright colours for impact.

Size
Card size 14cm (5½in) square, aperture 9cm (3½in) square

Yarn
Four-ply wool yarn – small amounts of assorted colours
Yarn left over from working other patterns in this book will be ideal for this purpose.

Needles
A pair of 4mm (US6, UK8) straight needles

Extras
Blank cards, preferably with pre-cut apertures, of a variety of colours, shapes and sizes
PVA

Tension
22 sts and 30 rows = 10cm (4in) over st st, after pressing

Note
- Read the charts from right to left for RS rows and left to right for WS rows.
- Use the Fair Isle technique to work the Christmas-tree and flower charts, stranding the yarn across the back of the work.
- Use the Fair Isle or the intarsia technique to work the cat chart, depending on your knitting preference and how you intend to embellish the design.

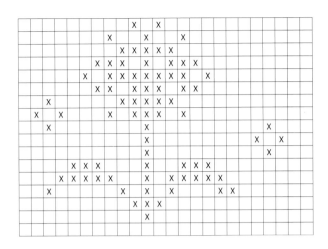
Flower chart.

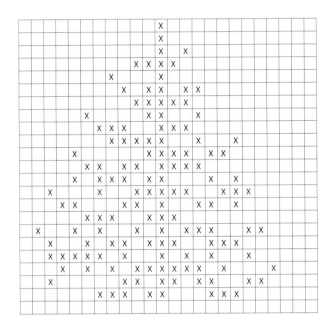
Christmas-tree chart.

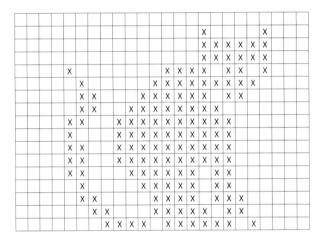
Cat chart.

Method
Work any of the charts that appear in this section with four to six stitches added on each side and extra rows added at the top and bottom of each piece of knitting, to allow it to overlap the inside of the card.

Finishing and making up
Embellish the knitted fabric with Swiss darning and embroidery as desired.

When the knitting has been completed, sew in all yarn tails, trim the ends and wash, block and press the fabric firmly. This will make the knitted pieces much easier to handle.

Add PVA on to the inside of the card around the aperture, and glue the knitted pieces carefully into place. Some cards have a backing; to attach it, place glue lightly all over the surface that will contact the knitted piece, because it is not desirable to have puddles of glue coming through to the right side of the knitting.

Leave the glue to dry completely before handling and writing in the cards.

Design your own

If you are not confident with drawing your own motifs from scratch, gain inspiration and guidance by looking at embroidery motifs, and work these into your own cards, using the Fair Isle or intarsia technique.

Bunting

Using a variety of colours and an i-cord, long or short lengths of bunting are fun to make. Place the flags closer together to create more of a flutter.

Size
Width × length, 13cm × 16cm (5in × 6½in)

Yarn
Rowan Cotton Glacé – small amounts of several bright shades
  Yarn left over from working other patterns in this book will be ideal for this purpose.

Needles
A pair of 3.25mm (US3, UK10) straight needles
A pair of 3.25mm (US3, UK10) dpns, for working the i-cord

Bunting on a boat at St Ives.

Tension
24 sts and 30 rows = 10cm (4in) over st st, after washing and pressing

Method
Using 3.25mm needles, cast on 32 sts, and work 8 rows st st. These rows will be later form a channel for the i-cord to be threaded through.
Row 1 K1, ssk, work to last 3 sts, k2tog, k1.
Rows 2–4 Work 3 rows st st.
Rep rows 1–4 until 4 sts remain.
Next rows Work 3 rows st st.
Next row Ssk, k2tog.
Cut the yarn, thread a tapestry needle with the yarn tail, pass the needle through the remaining stitches and draw the stitches together.

Make a total of twelve flags of various colours.
Make enough i-cord for the length of bunting required (*see* Appendix 1 for instructions to work this embellishment).

Finishing and making up
Sew in all yarn tails, and trim the ends.

Form the channel at the top of each flag by folding over the top 8 rows of st st and slip stitching the cast-on edge to the eighth row.

Thread the i-cord through the channel at the top of the flag, and stitch each flag in place by sewing through the channel and i-cord with a length of yarn. For the example, the flags were spaced 12cm (4¾in) apart.

Wash, block and firmly press each flag.

Design your own

Swiss-darn motifs on to the flags for a children's party, perhaps stars and teddy bears. For Christmas bunting, use red and green yarn. Use the colours of the bridesmaids and bouquets for wedding-celebration bunting.

CHAPTER 9

DESIGNING WITH COLOUR

Slip-stitch and butterfly-stitch variations

By studying one particular set of stitches and adapting and changing them in a variety of ways, you can really begin to gain confidence and start to design stitches of your own. The following instructions will take you on a journey by adding rows, stitches and colour to create different stitch patterns.

There are some amazingly versatile stitches, but, for this exercise, slip-stitch and butterfly-stitch (also known as coin stitch, as featured in the section 'Cafetière cosy and mug cosies' in Chapter 8) patterns have been chosen. These patterns can be used in multiple ways, by altering the number of stitches that are dropped and picked up, and, by changing yarn colours, a different style of fabric can be produced. The interest is in the textures created by the yarns weaving over and under each other.

Deciding what colour to use or change is a journey of discovery, and it is fun. Most people have a favourite colour and colour palette. Certain colours stimulate the memory or lift the mood, and the choices of colour can indicate a lot about the types of people we are.

The juxtaposing of colour and stitches is a lifelong learning experience. Wonderful tweedy, textured patterns can be introduced to the knitting, and, even when only one colour is used in each row, the overall effect can be rich in texture. Many colours can be added throughout a piece of fabric, or the stitch pattern can be used with a single colour only, from which beautiful, intricate, textured designs emerge.

When using more than one colour, and to make a neat edge, drop the yarn just used to the front of the work (the side closest to you), and pick up the new colour just behind it on the wrong side of the work. In this way, the yarn will be woven along the edge neatly.

The first set of variations is based on the butterfly stitch. For this stitch, 'butterfly' refers to the shape

OPPOSITE: Slip-stitch and butterfly-stitch variations.

Detail of a coin on the right side of the fabric.

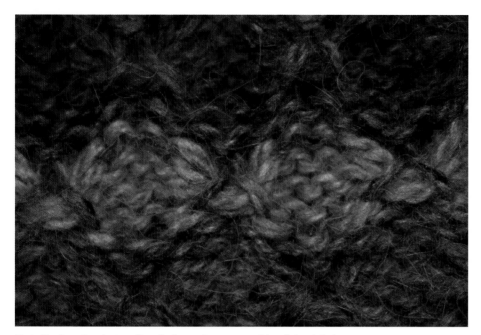

Details showing butterfly stitch on the wrong side of the fabric.

made by the stitches that are unravelled and then gathered up and knitted together as one, and the term 'coin' refers to the shape made by the remaining stitches, which are pulled into a round, slightly embossed shape.

Basic butterfly stitch

Sample 1
Worked over a multiple of 4 sts plus 3 sts.
The sample was worked with A = navy and B = blue.
With A, cast on.
Row 1 (WS) With A, p across.
Rows 2 and 4 With B, k across.
Rows 3 and 5 With B, p across.
Row 6 With A, k3, * drop the next st off the LH needle, unravel the st 4 rows down, pick up the A-coloured st from row 1 below, insert the RH needle into this st and under the four loose B-coloured yarn strands, knit the st (gathering up the four loose strands behind it), rep from * to the last 3 sts, k3.
Row 7 With A, p across.
Rows 8 and 10 With B, k across.
Rows 9 and 11 With B, p across.

Row 12 With A, k1, * drop the next st off the LH needle, unravel the st 4 rows down, pick up the A-coloured st from row 7 below with the LH needle, insert the RH needle into this st and under the four loose B-coloured yarn strands, knit the st, k3; rep from * to the last st, k1.
Rep rows 1–12.

Sample 2
The coin in this sample is larger; instead of 3 sts, as in sample 1, it is worked over 5 sts.
Worked over a multiple of 6 sts plus 3 sts.
The sample was worked with A = navy and B = green.
With A, cast on.
Rows 1–5 Work rows 1–5 of sample 1.
Row 6 (RS) With A, k1, * drop the next st off the LH needles, unravel the st 4 rows down, pick up the A-coloured st from row 1 below, insert the RH needle into this st and under the four loose B-coloured yarn strands, knit the st (gathering up the four loose strands behind it), k5; rep from * to the last st. K1.
Rows 7–11 Work rows 7–11 of sample 1.
Row 12 With A, k4, * drop the next st off the LH needle, unravel the st 4 rows down, pick up the A-coloured st from row 7 below with the LH needle, insert the RH needle into this st and under the four loose B-coloured yarn strands, knit the st, k5; rep from * to the last 4 sts. K4.
Rep rows 1–12.

Butterfly-stitch charts

Butterfly stitch can also be expressed with a chart, and the accompanying charts show how this would appear.

The X symbol indicates the unravelled stitches, and the & symbol denotes the butterfly stitch (the gathered stitches).

If you work through the stitch combinations, it will become clear how you can build up the size of the coin

Butterfly-stitch samples 1, 2 and 3.

Sample 1

+3	+2	+1	4	3	2	1	4	3	2	1	4	3	2	1
	&				&				&				&	
	X				X				X				X	
	X				X				X				X	
	X				X				X				X	
	X				X				X				X	
			&				&				&			
			X				X				X			
			X				X				X			
			X				X				X			
			X				X				X			

Butterfly-stitch sample 1 chart.

Sample 2

+3	+2	6	5	4	3	2	1	6	5	4	3	2	1	+1
	&			&						&				
	X			X						X				
	X			X						X				
	X			X						X				
	X			X						X				
							&						&	&
							X						X	X
							X						X	X
							X						X	X
							X						X	X

Butterfly-stitch sample 2 chart.

and change its shape through stitch, row and yarn-colour variations.

Sample 3

Worked over a multiple of 6 sts plus 3 sts.

The sample was worked with A = navy and B = peacock.

Worked as for sample 2, but the coins are longer, so work an extra 2 rows with B between the unravelled rows.

By now the sequence and rhythm of the stitch pattern will be clear. The coin can be made larger and smaller.

Sample 4

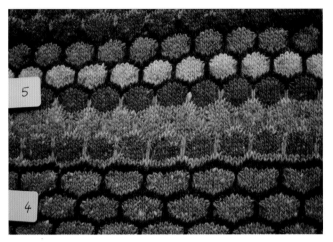

Butterfly-stitch samples 4 and 5.

Worked over a multiple of 8 sts plus 3 st(s).

The sample was worked with A = navy and B = brown.

The coins are larger, being worked across 7 sts with B and over 6 rows.

Sample 5

The coins are knitted across 5 sts, and the colour changes with each row of coins, and the colour of the rows in between the sets of unravelled rows also changes.

Sample 6

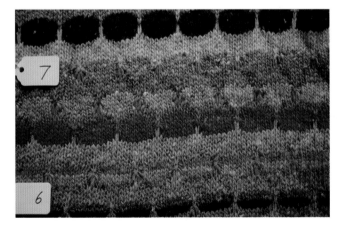

Butterfly-stitch samples 6 and 7.

The coins are worked across 7 sts, and the B colour changes three times.

Extra rows are knitted between the coins: the sample shows 4 rows worked with A. The B colour changes every 2 rows. So, the coins are multicoloured.

Sample 7

Using bright, fizzing colours, the coins are less pronounced, and a rhythm is set up, as the colours swing backwards and forwards.

The sample shows B as red worked over 6 rows, A as orange over 2 rows, B as yellow over 6 rows and A as bright blue over 2 rows.

Sample 8

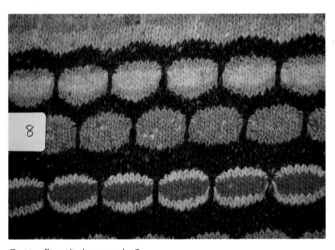

Butterfly-stitch sample 8.

This is a pattern that I have used many, many times. The coins morph into little tambourines, alive with movement dynamism. The plain navy throws the circles forwards and outlines the colour around the edges of the coins.

The sample shows 4 rows worked with A (navy). The B-coloured coins are worked over 7 sts and 8 rows, changing yarn colour after 2, 4 and 2 rows.

Sample 9

Playing and experimenting with one stitch pattern is

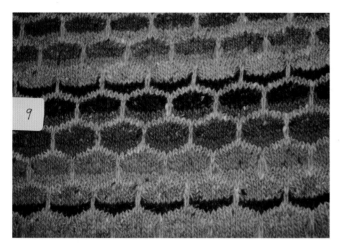

Butterfly-stitch sample 9.

Design your own

To design your own stitch, decide on the length of the dropped ladder, insert the LH needle into the corresponding stitch in the row below where the ladder is to end and unravel down to it. To achieve the butterfly effect, place the loose strands over the LH needle. When the RH needle knits the picked-up stitch at the base of the ladder, all of the strands are knitted together as one stitch. The gathered stitches give the impression of a butterfly.

great fun, and it enhances knowledge and understanding of stitch shape and how it can be manipulated. A simple technique can be developed into sophisticated colour patterns.

The sample shows A as a pale blue for 2 rows, and B changes colour after 2 and 4 rows. Each coin has a different colour change.

Colour-change slip-stitch patterns – hexagon shapes and wild variations

The second set of stitch patterns to study and explore is based on slip stitches, and it is a lifetime's work just experimenting and developing pattern formations from these basic stitches.

Threads can be drawn up, down and across, and the basic formula is relatively easy, so it is possible to really go to town with colour changing and altering scale. The fabric produced will be more dense than normal, as a characteristic of this stitch is that the slip stitches pull the other stitches together, to give a ruched appearance, which can make for exciting textures. Because of the vertical density of the stitches, more rows will need to be knitted to gain the desired length than would be necessary if knitting with, say, stocking stitch. This can also apply to the width, with more stitches being required to achieve the same width as a piece of stocking-stitch fabric: be aware that more stitches will be required. The fabric does not easily stretch out and will

feel knotted and taut. Keep your knitting tension and handling of the yarn strands loose and relaxed.

There are many variations from this one basic pattern, in which the slip stitches pull certain rows out of line upwards and downwards to form a hexagon. This shape can all but disappear when colours are added and stitches are manipulated.

To check whether a colour variation is working well, I find it helpful either to look at the fabric in a mirror or take a photograph of it and then view it that way. If the tones and shades are too close together and the pattern will therefore be lost, this will be evident when viewing the fabric in these ways. Contrariwise, if there is a glaring colour that dominates and unbalances the others, it will show clearly and can be rectified.

Slip-stitch sample 1.

These stitch patterns can also be expressed with charts, as with the previous stitch variations.

The technique for slipping stitches will specify 'with yarn in front' (wyif) or 'with yarn in back' (wyib). This does not refer to the right side or the wrong side of the fabric when it is finished, but it is in relation to the knitter. The front is towards or close to the knitter; the back is away from the knitter. After the stitch has been slipped, the yarn returns to the knit or purl position, depending on what the next stitch is to be.

The rule to remember with these slip-stitch patterns is that, on a knit row, for any slip stitch, the yarn is held at the back of the work and, on a purl row, at the front, unless stated otherwise.

Sample 1

Worked over a multiple of 8 sts plus 6 sts.

The sample was worked with A = purple and B = pale blue.

Row 1 With A, k across.

Row 2 With A, p across.

Note that, throughout the following 6 rows, the same A stitches are slipped.

Rows 3, 5 and 7 With B, k2, * sl 2 sts wyib, k6; rep from * to the last 4 sts, sl 2 sts, k2.

Rows 4, 6 and 8 With B, p2, * sl 2 sts wyif, p6; rep from * to the last 4 sts, sl 2 sts, p2.

Row 9 With A, k across.

Row 10 With A, p across.

Row 11, 13 and 15 With B, k6, * sl 2 sts wyib, k6; rep from * to end.

Row 12, 14 and 16 With B, p6, * sl 2 sts wyif, p6; rep from * to end.

Rep rows 1–16.

All the other slip-stitch patterns are based on this sample. By altering the number of rows that are worked and the stitches that are slipped, a huge archive of stitch variations can be developed.

Sample 2

Depending on the yarn-colour choice, the effect of this pattern can resemble a Florentine pattern or peacock feathers.

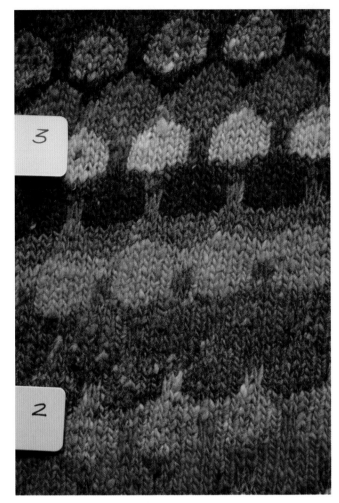

Slip-stitch samples 2 and 3.

Rows 1–8 Work rows 1–8 of sample 1.

Rows 9–10 Work rows 9–10 of sample 1 with B.

Change to C for rows 11–16, 1 and 2.

Rep rows 3–16.

Sample 3

The basic sample 1 is used for this pattern, but the colours of the hexagons change, as well as the colours of the rows in between the hexagons. So, A changes every 2 rows and B every 6 rows.

Sample 4

A smaller, more intricate-looking pattern.

Rows 3 and 4 With B, work across, while slipping every fourth st.

Rows 5, 6, 7 and 8 With C, work across, while slipping the same sts as were slipped on the previous rows.

Row 9 With C, k across.

Row 10 With C, p across.

These 10 rows and colour changes form the pattern repeat.

Offset the slip stitches on the next pattern repeat.

Sample 6

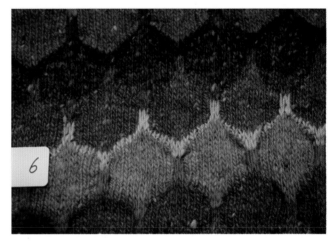

Slip-stitch sample 6.

Slip-stitch samples 4 and 5.

With A, knit 1 row, then purl 1 row.

With B as the working yarn, 1 st is slipped while 3 sts and 4 rows make up the basic hexagon, which now appears to be squarer in shape.

Sample 5

The busy, complicated appearance of this pattern is misleading. It is all produced by colour changing, specifically by the rows on which the colours are changed. It is a variation of sample 4.

To the 4 slip rows are added 2 rows worked with a contrasting colour, so there are 6 slip rows in total.

Row 1 With A, k across.

Row 2 With A, p across.

This pattern features a definite honeycomb shape.

The hexagon is worked over 10 sts and 12 rows, with 2 sts being slipped between the hexagons, so this really is extreme knitting.

The colours are changed for each hexagon and for the rows where there are no slip stitches between the hexagons. Do not pull the yarn taut over this pattern; it should be used gently and flow through your hands easily.

Sample 7

This is a mosaic pattern. All of the rows in this pattern feature slip stitches: there are no plain rows in between the hexagons.

The hexagon is worked over 10 sts, with 2 sts being slipped in between the hexagons.

Slip-stitch sample 7.

Rows 1–8 Work rows 1–8 of sample 1 with A.
Rows 9–16 Work rows 9–16 of sample 1 with B.
Offset the next hexagon over the next 16 rows, with 8 rows being worked with C and 8 rows with D.

Sample 8

Slip-stitch sample 8.

The pattern is based on sample 2, with 2 sts being slipped. The hexagon is formed of 6 sts , over 8 rows, with a colour change after row 4. The effect is a distorted egg shape, with the colour changing halfway through it.

   Worked over a multiple of 8 sts plus 6 sts.

Sample 9

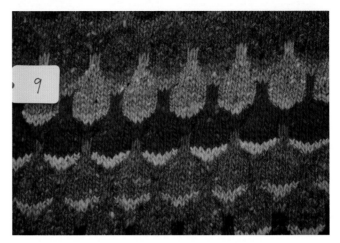

Slip-stitch sample 9.

Also based on the previous stitch pattern, this has a wonderful feathery effect, produced through colour changing. For this pattern, 2 sts are slipped, and the oval shape is made over 6 sts and 10 rows, with the first 2 rows being knitted with a different colour.

Covered boxes

Having completed or at least experimented and had fun playing around with the variety of butterfly and slip-stitch patterns, it is now time to make something

Design your own

By now, you will be confident working this stitch and able to design your own colour combinations and stitch variations.
Make lengths of these samples as an archive, and remember to write down carefully what process you followed so that, at a later date, if required, you are able to replicate the stitch. This is important: you think that you will remember, but, from my experience, you will not!

Stack of the pebbles, blue-mosaic and meadow-flowers boxes.

with them. While you could make cushion covers or throws by sewing all of your samples together, I chose to cover some boxes.

My intention for this project was both to make a useful object for storage and really go to town with a colour exercise.

Size
To fit a box, 34cm (13½in) square, with a lid

Yarn
Any 4ply yarn can be used in a variety of colours – approximately 400g.

Pebbles box
Colours A, B, C, D, E and F

Meadow-flowers box
At least colours A, B, C, D, E and F

Blue-mosaic box
Colours A, B, C, D

Needles
A pair of 3.25mm (US3, UK10) straight needles

Extras
Box, 34cm (13½in) square, with a lid
Elastic cord

Tension
28 sts and 36 rows = 10cm (4in) over st st, after pressing

Pebbles box

A collapsible box with a lid was bought, and the choice of colours and pattern were decided upon.

The pebbles box, while being useful, is also a sculpture of shapes, texture and colour. It can be reminiscent of a snowy landscape, a sea mist rising or a beach of fine sand. The aim was to create an abstract piece

Detail of the colours of the pebbles box.

with no borders; think beyond the knitting, and create with head, heart and hand. This is the true craft and art of knitting.

Rocks, waves, melting snow, and mist on the hills are all tangible scenes that can be poured into the art of knitting. Donegal-wool yarn, with its distinctive flecks and freckles of colour, also known as nepps, is useful when creating a scene, as are Shetland yarns and Rowan Felted Tweed, because they already contain a subtle mixture of colours.

The stitch pattern for the pebbles box is based on slip-stitch sample 8.

Worked over a multiple of 8 sts plus 6 sts.
Worked with yarn colours A, B, C, D, E and F.
Row 1 With A, k across.
Row 2 With A, p across.
Note that, throughout the following 8 rows, the same A stitches are slipped.
Rows 3 and 5 With B, k2, * sl 2 sts wyib, k6; rep from * to the last 4 sts, sl 2 sts, k2.
Rows 4 and 6 With B, p2, * sl 2 sts wyif, p6; rep from * to the last 4 sts, sl 2 sts, p2.
Rows 7 and 9 With C, rep row 3.
Rows 8 and 10 With C, rep row 4.
Row 11 With D, k across.
Row 12 With D, p across.
Rows 13 and 15 With E, k6, * sl 2 sts wyib, k6; rep from * to end.
Rows 14 and 16 With E, p6, * sl 2 sts wyif, p6; rep from * to end.
Rows 17 and 19 With F, rep row 13.
Rows 18 and 20 With F, rep row 14.
Rep rows 1–20 with different yarn colours.

Meadow-flowers box

The meadow-flowers box features the same stitch pattern as the pebbles box, but the colours are those of summer flowers: reds, purples, cerise, yellow, emerald and turquoise, to name just a few. Use all of the bright colours that you can find; the more clashing the better. The piece created can have an energy and fizz, a crackle and pop, and be a thoroughly enjoyable experience to work, which in turn can make the soul sing.

Meadow-flowers box.

Blue-mosaic box

The slip-stitch pattern used for this box creates a more textured, ruched and wavy fabric, based on slip-stitch sample 7, with yarns of blues, greens, ochres and purples. The overall effect, after pressing, is of mosaic tiles. Keep the tension loose, and use larger needles if necessary, to avoid the work becoming too tight.

The pattern is worked over 24 sts.

Worked with yarn colours A, B, C and D, and so on.

Rows 1, 3 and 5 With A, k5, * sl 2 sts wyib, k10; rep from * to the last 5 sts, k5.

Blue-mosaic box.

Rows 2, 4 and 6 With A, p5, * sl 2 sts wyif, k10; rep from * to the last 5 sts, p5.

Rows 7, 9 and 11 With B, rep row 1.

Rows 8, 10 and 12 With B, rep row 2.

Rows 13, 15 and 17 With C, k1, * k10, sl 2 sts wyib; rep from * to the last st, k1.

Rows 14, 16 and 18 With C, k1, * k10, sl 2 sts wyif; rep from * to the last st, k1.

Rows 19, 21 and 23 With D, rep row 13.

Rows 20, 22 and 24 With D, rep row 14.

Rep rows 1–24 with various yarn colours.

Method (all boxes)

Gather all of the colours of yarn together that are to be used, and work a tension swatch, to enable you to work out the number of stitches to cast on and rows to work. Wash, block and press the swatch: it will be quite textured, and the fabric needs to settle before it is measured.

Having measured the depth of the box, cast on the required number of stitches, based on the measurements of your tension swatch. Work enough fabric to stretch around and fully cover the four sides of the box, and cast off. For the 34cm (13½in)-square boxes shown, 110 sts were cast on and 784 rows were worked.

For the lid, cast on the number of stitches required to create a piece of fabric that will stretch across the width of the top of the lid, from one side to the other (excluding the depth of the lid's rim).

Work enough rows for the length of the fabric to go from the bottom of the rim on one side of the lid to the bottom rim on the opposite side of the box.

Cast off.

Finishing and making up (all boxes)

Sew in all yarn tails, trim the ends and wash, block and lightly press the fabric, without flattening the texture.

For the box covering, sew together the cast-on and cast-off edges, and thread elastic cord through the edges of the two long sides, which will be positioned at the top and bottom of the sides of the box.

Pull the fabric over the box, so that the elastic is positioned just above and just below the top and bottom

Design your own

Think about using cables and basket twisted stitches. For a child's play box, make squares worked with intarsia or Swiss darn letters or animals in the middle of the blocks of colour, then sew the squares together. Cover waste paper baskets with a fabric of restrained stripes in shades of neutral colours or to match your interior.

of the sides, which will pull in the work just under the base and over the top rim of the box.

To complete the lid, depending on how deep the rim of the lid is, say, 3cm (1¼in), with the right side of the fabric facing you, start picking up stitches 3cm (1¼in) up from the cast-on end of one long side edge of the fabric, stopping 3cm (1¼in) down from the cast-off end of that side edge.

Work the stitch pattern until the fabric is of the same length as the depth of the rim. Cast off.

Repeat picking up stitches and working a short length of fabric for the opposite long side edge of the fabric.

Sew the pairs of adjacent side seams together, to give shape to the fabric when it is pulled on over the lid.

Thread elastic cord through the bottom circumference of the lid fabric, and pull the fabric over the lid. The edges of the fabric should sit nicely along the bottom of the lid rim and not tuck under it, because the thickness of the knitted fabric may prevent the box lid from fitting properly over the top of the box.

Conclusion

To start to think about designing your own knitted projects, look at nature: everything comes from nature and its colour palette. Start with the colours for your project; these are the catalyst for the choice of stitch pattern, to create a dynamic energy and rhythm, allowing some of the colours to push forwards while others recede. Make use of the quality of the yarn: a primary colour of Donegal-wool yarn with flecks will result in a softer finish than that of a DK merino yarn, which will be sharper.

Many stitch patterns lend themselves to colour experimentation. A rigid plan is not always necessary, especially when making throws, blankets and cushions. Start working, and add colours to enhance or moderate others as you proceed. Working this way requires a lot of thought and can be meditative. Even when working with familiar stitches and motifs, push the boundaries to keep your work fresh. Try adding unfamiliar colours or stitches. Mix cables with Fair Isle patterns or twisted stitches, and mix intarsia with slip stitches.

One project will lead on to another. Allow time for designs to develop, by laying aside a work in progress for a few days, to be able to view it again with fresh eyes. Your mood, the light and many other factors will have changed, and this may, in turn, lead on to another creative development.

Whatever you are working on, enjoy it, as this is the essence of working with your head, heart and hand.

EMBELLISHMENTS AND ADDITIONS

I-Cord

An i-cord is knitted with dpns. Depending on the thickness of cord required, cast on three to five stitches, and knit across the row.

Without turning the work, slide the stitches to the opposite end of the needle that they are sitting on.

Pull the yarn firmly from the end of the row across to the right, then knit across the row: this forces the stitches to form a circle, which, after a few rows of knitting, form a tube of fabric.

Repeat this process of sliding the stitches, pulling across the yarn and knitting another row, until you have the desired length of cord.

Tassels

Decide on the length of the tassel, and cut a sturdy piece of card of the same length.

Wrap the yarn that will form the tassel around the card multiple times, keeping the wraps of yarn parallel to each other and close together.

Thread a needle with a long strand of yarn, insert the needle underneath all of the wrapped strands of yarn on the front of the card, by sliding the needle against the card's surface, and pull the strand through to the opposite side of the wrapped strands, leaving a tail of yarn available on the side that the needle was inserted.

Tie two basic overhand knots in the strand of yarn, to tightly gather and secure the wraps of yarn together. The knots should be positioned close to one end of the strand, leaving a long length of yarn available. If the yarn keeps breaking when it is tied tightly, use dental floss instead.

With scissors, make a perpendicular cut through the wrapped strands of yarn, at the furthest point possible from the knotted strand that is gathering the wraps of yarn: this will ensure that the threads of the tassel are all of equal length. This releases the tassel from the card.

A length of i-cord.

A tassel.

Keeping the tassel threads gathered together and arranged as they were when on the card, wrap the long tail of the knotted strand around the head of the tassel multiple times, close to where the tassel threads are folded over and gathered, to form a shank. Insert the long tail of the strand through the small loop at the top of the tassel (between the knotted strand and the just-made wraps of yarn forming the head of the tassel), to secure it.

Pom-poms

Pom-pom makers are available that really speed up the process of creating pom-poms. However, stiff card can be used instead.

Cut out two identical circular pieces of card of the required diameter of the pom-pom. Cut a hole in the centre of each circle: the circles should be of the same size.

Holding the two pieces of card together as a double layer and in alignment, wrap yarn around the cards, starting by passing the ball of yarn through the centre of the circle, over the top of the cards, under the cards, and back up through the centre of the circle, until the hole in the middle has nearly disappeared by being filled with wraps of yarn. Aim to cover the entire surface of the cards, evenly, to create a dense pom-pom.

Cut through all of the wrapped yarn, by carefully inserting the tip of a pair of scissors between the two adjacent card circles and following the perimeter of the cards.

Guide a strand of yarn between the two adjacent card circles, and wrap the strand entirely around all of the wrapped strands of yarn. Tie two basic overhand knots in this strand to secure it firmly around the wrapped strands. If the yarn is soft and breaks, use dental floss instead: it is strong and almost invisible.

Remove the card circles.

Finished pom-poms as embellishments.

Swiss darning

Also known as duplicate stitch.

This a very useful technique that can be used to embellish knitted fabric and even cover up mistakes!

A pom-pom in the making.

Swiss darning in progress.

The effect is to cover up a stitch that has been knitted.

Thread a needle with the length of yarn to be used for the Swiss darning, secure the thread on the back of the work, and bring the needle to the front of the work at the base of the stitch to be covered (at the very base of the V of the knit stitch as seen from the front of the work).

Insert the needle from right to left behind the knit stitch above the knit stitch to be covered: the needle will pass horizontally behind both the diagonal legs of the V of the stitch above.

Take the needle down through the base of the knit stitch to be covered to the back of the work: this is the same point that the needle came up through when starting to Swiss-darn the stitch.

Take the needle to the front of the work again, bringing it up at the base of the next knit stitch to be covered.

Detail of crocheted edgings.

Swiss darning being worked across Fair Isle patterns.

Double-crochet edging

This is a great way to finish the edges of your work, and it is a simple way of including extra or contrasting colours that add another dimension to the finished project.

Secure the yarn to form the crocheted edging on the back of the work.

From the front of the fabric, insert the crochet hook between two knitted stitches one row down from the edge of the fabric, and pull a loop of yarn through from the back of the work to the front.

Working from right to left, insert the crochet hook into the next gap between two stitches, and again pull a loop of yarn through from the back of the work to the front : there will now be two loops of yarn held on the crochet hook.

Pass the yarn over the hook from right to left, and pull the yarn through the two loops held on the crochet hook: this completes the formation of the first crocheted stitch.

Continuing to work from right to left, insert the hook into the next gap between two stitches, and repeat the previous steps of pulling through a loop of yarn twice, passing the yarn over the hook and pulling that yarn through the two held loops on the hook.

Work entirely around the perimeter of the knitted fabric, adding three extra, adjacent stitches at any corners, to enable the edging to lie flat and not be pulled out of shape. Alternatively, work along the entire length of two opposite edges, such as the short ends of a rug, for a different edging effect.

Add additional rows of crochet if required, with the same colour of yarn or with a contrasting yarn colour.

Blanket stitch

Blanket stitch creates a small and delicate edging.

Thread a needle with the contrast-colour yarn to form the blanket-stitch edging, secure the yarn on the

Blanket-stitch edging being worked.

Working from right to left, insert the needle again from the front to the back of the fabric two stitches away from the first needle-insertion point, ensuring that the yarn running from the last stitch is lying behind the needle, running from right to left, then pull on the needle gently until the yarn forms a stitch that lies against the surface of the front of the fabric, perpendicular to the fabric's edge.

Continuing to work from right the left, again insert the needle two stitches along, from the front to the back, with the yarn lying behind the needle, running from the last stitch, before pulling the needle and yarn through gently to form a stitch on the surface of the fabric.

back of the work and insert the needle from the front to the back one row down from the edge of the fabric, between two stitches.

A final piece of inspiration: the colours of Harris.

FURTHER READING

Knitting handbooks

A good source for these books is charity shops: look in the crafts section. Some of these books are out of print, so you could also try finding them at www.abebooks.com.

Dupernex, A., *Beginner's Guide to Knitting* (Search Press, 2004)
Mon Tricot, *1100 Stitch Patterns* (Condé Nast Publications, 1978)
Rutt, R., *A History of Hand Knitting* (Batsford, 1987)
Thomas, M., *Mary Thomas's Knitting Book* (Hodder and Stoughton, 1938)
Walker, B., *A Second Treasury Of Knitting Patterns* (Schoolhouse Press, 1998)
Walker, B., *A Treasury Of Knitting Patterns* (Schoolhouse Press, 1998)

Craftsmanship

Frayling, C., *On Craftsmanship, towards a new Bauhaus* (Oberon Books, 2011)
Pye, D., *The Nature And Art Of Workmanship* (Cambridge University Press, 1968)

Colour

Baty, P., *The Anatomy Of Colour* (Thames and Hudson, 2017)
de Sausmarez, J., *Basic Colour: a practical handbook* (A&C Black, 2008)
Lawson, I., *From The Land Comes The Cloth* (Ian Lawson Books, 2013): a stunning book with evocative and mesmerizing photographs of the Hebrides. It is large and expensive, so borrow it from the library.
Nicholson, J., *Winifred Nicholson in Cumberland* (Abbot Hall Art Gallery, 2016): exhibition guide
Riley, B., *The Eye's Mind: Bridget Riley* (Thames and Hudson, 1999)

CONTACTS AND SUPPLIERS

Yarns

Rowan Yarns
Green Lane Mill, Holmfirth, West Yorkshire, England HD9 2DX
www.knitrowan.com

Knoll Yarns Limited
1 Wells Road, Ilkley, West Yorkshire, LS29 9JB
www.knollyarns.com

Haberdashery, feather cushion pads and collapsible boxes

Dunelm, www.dunelm.com
John Lewis, www.johnlewis.com

INDEX